LEADERS WITH A HEART - VOLUME II

FEATURING GOOSEBUMP-INDUCING STORIES OF ENLIGHTENED SOULS DISCOVERING THEIR GIFT AND SHARING IT AROUND THE WORLD

Divine Destiny Publishing

Copyright © 2024 by Divine Destiny Publishing and Mary Gooden

All Rights Reserved. Apart from any fair dealing for the purposes of research or private study, or criticism or review, as permitted under the Copyright, Designs and Patents Act 1988, this publication may only be reproduced, stored or transmitted, in any form or by any means, with the prior permission in writing of the copyright owner, or in the case of the reprographic reproduction in accordance with the terms of licensees issued by the Copyright Licensing Agency. Enquiries concerning reproduction outside those terms should be sent to the publisher.

CONTENTS

Introduction	v
1. Jay Lee *Unveiling The Sales Ninja Within*	1
Episode 32	11
2. Mary Gooden *Every Experience is a Gift to Inspire Another*	13
Episode 55	25
3. Kim Wagner *Stepping Into Your Greatness*	26
Episode 65 & 70	37
4. Payman Lorenzo *Identify And Share Your Gifts With The World*	38
Episode 100, 283 & 300	49
5. Anaiis Salles *Love Your YES and Live It!*	51
Episode 154 & 298	65
6. Amanda Lindsey *Spreading Happiness: My Gift to the World and Its Gift to Me*	67
Episode 180 & 290	81
7. Tucker Stine *I Am Not Lost, Just Re-found*	83
Episode 213	91
8. Marcus Snowden iBallin® w/Snow *Play Locally...Win Globally*	93
Episode 233 & 300	107
9. Brittany Rychlik *In Touch With the Wild Side*	109
Episode 255	119
10. Leslie Sloane *How an Auracle Consultation Can Help You Get Back On Track*	120

Episodes 262, 264, 281 & 293   131
11. About The Publisher   133
Divine Destiny Publishing and Mary Gooden

INTRODUCTION

From a very early age, I've always wanted to help, connect, empower, and inspire others. At the start of 2020 I returned to Canada, leaving Hong Kong, a place I loved and considered my home, I asked myself a powerful question: "What can I do that will allow me to help, bring together and connect people while inspiring and empowering them to do good so that together we can inspire others to do good as well?" That's when my podcast, Leaders With A Heart, was born in October of 2020. Little did I know that this would turn out to be, one of the most impactful and life changing decisions of my life so far!

My Podcast and Youtube Channel are a platform to show case purpose driven entrepreneurs who have a beautiful heart, a powerful message and goosebump inducing stories to share their gifts with the world. So that we can inspire and empower others to do good in order to create a better world together, one entrepreneur at a time.

Fast forward to now, over three years and three hundred and ten episodes later and counting. It's been nothing short of life changing and countless blessings. I have been blessed with the honour of connecting with incredible people from all walks of life, all true experts in their respective industries and sectors, and all having one thing in common: being heart centred and doing good, around them and around the world. In their own unique ways.

It is my utmost honour to call these truly enlightened souls, not only guests in my podcasts but, most importantly, my dear friends. Indeed, having had wonderful heart to heart conversations with them, we've been able to connect at a much deeper level.

I am honoured to bring some of these stories to you. These are truly empowering, inspiring, impactful, and powerful stories. Stories of every day people, purpose driven and true Leaders With A Heart, identifying, embracing and then, sharing their GIFTS around them and around the world. There are so many other stories that could have easily been in this book but for various reasons, didn't, mostly due to timing. However, the good news is, that this is the second volume!

We all, no exception, have our own unique Gifts. These can be unique skills that we may have been born with. Or they could also be, lessons, wisdoms and experiences we've accumulated in this lifetime.

We all know that life is a school. We come here to learn, grow and become a better, wiser person. However, that's only five to ten percent of why we are here. The remaining ninety to ninety five percent is taking those gifts, those lessons and wisdoms we've learned on our path so far and sharing them with others so that we can all learn, grow and ultimately, we can all collectively rise.

This is what Volume II, the book you have in your hands, is all about. Purpose driven, impact driven, heart centred leaders, leaders with a heart, sharing their gifts with us so that we can all learn, grow and benefit from. Through this, we can create a massive movement, an unstoppable waive and ripple effect worldwide.

May these stories inspire you to identify, embrace and share your very own GIFTS so that you can do good in your own unique, beautiful, and special way, to make the world around you a better place.

Godspeed,

Payman Lorenzo, Da Nang, Vietnam, January 2024.

JAY LEE

UNVEILING THE SALES NINJA WITHIN

In the vast tapestry of life, my journey from an introverted banker and pastor grappling with Imposter Syndrome, limiting beliefs, procrastination, low self-esteem, and a voice stifled by insecurity, is a testament to the transformative power of discovering and sharing one's unique gift. Growing up in Toronto, Canada, in an immigrant family that valued hard work over handouts, my trajectory seemed predetermined. Yet life had an unexpected pivot awaiting me—a shift from pastoring to becoming a profitability rainmaker. The underdog "zero to hero" story unfolded as I navigated financial struggles, learning resilience from my tenacious parents.

The first turning point came when I unearthed my God-given gift of connecting with people. Rooted in over forty thousand conversations sharing the gospel, and witnessing over ten thousand conversions, my journey from brokenness to becoming a sought-after speaker on podcasts, summits, and live events mirrors the alchemy of transformation.

My transformation from an underdog, battling self-doubt and insecurity, to a thriving "Sales Ninja," armed with the *Reverse G.L.A.S.S. Selling Method*, is a testament to the power of discovering and sharing one's unique gift. In this metamorphosis, I discovered a second gift—the art of sales. Trained by the late Korby Waters, a "10-figure" sales closer, I honed my skills, achieving up to eighty-one percent close rates and ninety-six percent cash collected rates, the highest on every high-ticket sales team I joined. Notably, my prowess extended to closing for renowned coaches like Akbar Sheikh, Vince Delmonte, Nick Kozmin, Corey Davis, Tuan Nguyen, and Facebook scaling ads expert, Nick Guadagnano.

The Birth of the Sales Ninja

The idea of having a gift, particularly in sales, seemed very foreign to me considering I was an introvert. Never in a million years did I dream that I would be a high ticket sales coach, speaking in front of thousands of people. So, the impossible became possible. The unlikely became likely. My primary message and motivator to help others is the understanding of "being faithful with little and entrusted with much." And so, through my own financial struggles, my gift was revealed. I am here to help others break the cycle of generational poverty by sharing this gift of sales, so they can believe the impossible and, with real results, radically transform their lives, families, and friends.

I believe this mission chose me because there are so many people in my shoes. The quiet and reserved are often overlooked and become the underdogs. Learning how to find your voice and secure your identity can unleash the "Sales Ninja" in anyone—you can *Ninjafy* your level of life and income in ways you've never experienced before. I truly believe I can transform lives and gladly accept the mission to achieve this in my lifetime.

I am embarrassed to share this next story but I do so with the sole purpose to help all the underdogs and voiceless ones out there to know your identity and discover your voice, to fight back and be who God has called you to be, and to do all that God has gifted you to do.

In Grade Four, my teacher was not the nicest teacher. I don't know about her childhood or what challenges she was facing on that snowy, cold day in December, but she would not listen to my simple request. I was raised, in a good family with amazing parents, to always respect my teachers and elders. I was taught not to argue back or fight back, but to take the blame for pretty much everything. Now, I realize this is not the healthiest way to live life, but it was how I was raised and I followed the rules.

I looked out of the classroom window, gazing in awe at each unique snowflake, as the first snowfall in December came down so peacefully. Suddenly, I had the urge to go to the washroom and raised my hand to ask for permission. My teacher flat out told me I couldn't go until recess, which was at least fifteen minutes away. Now that seems like a short time, but when you have a small bladder like I did, raising my hand was not because I *kind of* had to go, but rather, I *really* had to go. I wasn't sure how I was going to make it to recess, so after a few minutes, I raised my hand again to ask for permission to go to the washroom. This time, my teacher was beyond furious and yelled back at me, as if I committed a heinous crime, and told me to put my hand down and wait for recess. She silenced me. I lost my voice. I lost my confidence and self esteem. My interruption was not only an inconvenience to her, but I was becoming a nuisance. Someone who was a straight-A student almost skipping two grades, who never caused or got into trouble. This situation caused great stress on my body because I had never been yelled at by a teacher. At this point, I was desperate and paced back and forth at the back of the classroom trying to find a way to get to the washroom. I looked outside to see it had started snowing heavily, then the weight of my urgency caused me to squeeze my legs together to stop the pressure—but I could no longer hold it.

It was as if time froze, and the snowflakes fell in slow motion. I had no voice. I was silenced. I was unsure of my identity. An introvert who couldn't speak up for myself, I wasn't able to stand up and fight for a simple human act of being. I was shut down and defeated. As I faced my demise, I felt utterly hopeless and in that moment; after holding on for what seemed like an eternity, I peed my pants. The grief and overwhelming wave of shame hit me like a ton of bricks, and I never felt lower in my entire life.

I could have let that moment in time and event of shame define me, but I refused to let that trauma control me. Instead, I decided to fight back. I mustered all of my competitive ability to overcome every obstacle, to silence all the naysayers, to demolish any hurdles, and to annihilate anyone who came up against me to tell me what I could or could not do.

This traumatic event was the turning point that lit a fuse in my spirit and fuelled my fire to use the gift of transformational leadership—which many people know as "Sales"—to help navigate people who are hurt, who are overwhelmed with anxiety and fear, who have been abused, neglected, overlooked, or who have been the underdog facing defeat over and over again. My mission and gift in life was, and is, to help the underdogs overcome adversity, to help empower them to discover their gift from God, to take their mess and transform it into a message or gift, to touch the world.

Staying Aligned with My Purpose in a Busy World

People often ask me how I have the energy to have taken sales calls for eight-to-ten hours per day, as a lot of energy is required to perform at the highest levels. I have several tips and hacks I'd like to share with you to help me perform at the highest elite levels. My daily routine involves meditation, reading Scriptures, prayer, exercise, positive affirmations, work outs in three areas—power, speed, flexibility—supplements, protein, liquid collagen, sublingual vitamin sprays, and reading. After all, "leaders are readers."

Let's talk about physical fitness.

This may sound unbelievable, but I work out up to three times a day, six-to-seven days each week. So, on a great week, I'll workout fourteen times! Obsessive? Maybe. Crazy? Probably. But one thing I do know is that I am disciplined and focused to have laser focus in regards to my health.

For cardio, I do ten-minute wind sprints one or two times per week, and play competitive volleyball every Monday. I also practice my golf swing daily, and with lessons, (hire a coach, thank me later), I have increased my drive and increased my distance from a measly 160-yard slice to hitting a 305-yard draw and landing on the green on a par 4 hole. My goal is now to hit 400-yards and break a score of 80. Crazy high goals? Yes. But I manifest and shift my mindset, coupled with faith and actions; I put in the work to bridge the gap to see these dreams come to fruition and become a reality. And so far, it's worked out really well.

I take a bunch of supplements, such as sublingual vitamin sprays, that go straight into my bloodstream. These also include energy and pain relief sprays, and a medical grade liquid collagen peptide that I drink almost daily for improved skin and bone density. My nails and hair grow almost twice as fast which is kind of annoying, but I know it works. I take protein whey and energy drinks which remove brain fog and bring laser focus clarity to help me get the deep work in.

I know my body and how much sleep I need. I'm functioning okay with five hours' sleep; when I get six or more hours, I slay the day. My *Oura* ring religiously tells me my ready score, sleep score, and activity score. The key to biohacking is understanding how your body works and optimizing the efficiency so you can be effective and lethal in all you do, whether it's in business, sports, or relationships.

Usually, I "sleep cold," meaning I don't wear anything except my boxers, and use minimal blankets. This ensures my body is in "preservation mode" and my resting heart rate while sleeping, when optimal, is usually in the forty-eight-to-fifty beats-per-minute range. I have friends who are in the low forties; they're savages. Marathon runners are in the thirties and forties but I'm not quite there yet. I also try to avoid water and or food three hours before I sleep, and to reduce screen time, but I'm not always successful with this.

My biggest kryptonite— that I am working on to this day—is going to sleep and waking up earlier. Ideally, I'd like to sleep by 10pm and wake up by 4 or 5am. Typically, I sleep well after midnight, so this is definitely a work in progress. Lord help me. I don't have problems falling asleep, I have problems with stopping work or doing other things because I have so much energy and so many ideas on how to transform lives by scaling businesses that I have a hard time shutting down.

Results Show Proof

At first, I wasn't much of a talker as I preferred to show by actions rather than my words. So I let my results do most of the talking. Recently I was listening to a podcast of one of the top sales closers who was training other sales reps, and learned she was closing twenty thousand dollars per week. I have been able to close over a hundred thousand dollars in ten days, and over one million dollars in ninety days, while working part-time. I even had a "9-Figure" Sales Coach and one of the top "sales jedis" on the planet, interview me on his podcast to understand how I was achieving these kinds of numbers.

The understanding I gained during my past life as a pastor and missionary, about giving first, adding value, and serving others first, was a large part of achieving these results. My faith in God and the actions I took while keeping my head down and focused on running in my own lane were also important in the success I achieved. At the time, I thought nothing of this because I wasn't aware of what others were doing. My only competition was against myself as I strived to become a better version of myself.

The Reverse G.L.A.S.S. Selling Method

The pinnacle of my revelation was the development of the *Reverse G.L.A.S.S. Selling Method*—an unparalleled approach that defies conventional sales methods. This method, rooted in biblical principles like giving first and serving with humility, shattered objections effortlessly, propelling me to close over one million dollars in just ninety days, part-time.

The G.L.A.S.S. Selling Method became my guiding star:

G - GIVE FIRST

I embraced the essence of *1 Peter 3:15*, approaching each call with gentleness and respect. The mantra "give first" became my modus operandi—providing value that moved the needle in their business or brought transformative change to their lives. Testimonials and case studies served as beacons, illuminating my ability to deliver massive results.

L - LISTEN WELL

Sales transformed into transformational leadership, shifting my focus from pitching to putting prospects first. Humility eclipsed ego as I recognized not all sales or clients were good. Every call became an opportunity to help another make the best decision for them—a decision they already wanted but needed clarity on.

A - ASK OPEN PIERCING QUESTIONS

Curiosity became my ally as I asked open piercing questions, unraveling deeper insights into prospects' needs and desires. Open questions like "What?" and "Why?" became the keys to understanding, steering away from the simplicity of closed questions that could halt the conversation.

S - SINCERELY HANDLE OBJECTIONS

Objections ceased to be obstacles and became opportunities for understanding. Instead of defensively viewing objections as negative events, I embraced them with sincerity. I reframed objections, urging prospects to consider the broader landscape rather than being swayed by isolated experiences.

S - SERVE WITH HUMILITY

In the spirit of humility, I shed the sales hat and donned the mantle of a servant, treating prospects as brothers and sisters. Acknowledging faults, miscommunication, and misinformation, I took responsibility by fostering an environment where people felt heard, understood, and cared for.

Understanding the gift of transformational leadership, which many of you call "sales," is simply helping people who are interested to make a buying decision they already want to make. Your gift is to help educate them, which brings understanding. It's not to convince, coerce, or manipulate them with a salesy, sleazy tactic. Rather, it is a beautiful way of listening first, giving value, and helping remove barriers and obstacles to help them move from their current state to their desired state or, even better, their dream state. Sales is the most powerful gift that one can possess. It changes the world. Sales is my God-given gift and I'm on a mission to use it so I don't lose it.

I invite you to envision your own metamorphosis. Embrace the journey from self-doubt to empowerment. You too can discover and share your unique gift so you can become a Sales Ninja and "sell more to give more." I want you to feel encouraged, empowered, inspired, motivated to act, even moved to tears. I want your life to be radically transformed. I want you to be financially free and flexible to live life on your own terms, and for all this to impact your families, friends, and communities, so they can sell more to give more to causes and projects that are near and dear to your hearts.

Join my FREE Facebook Group Community at www.facebook.com/groups/salesninjacommunity and schedule a complimentary *Sales Ninja* Audit call at call.gosalesninja.com/jlee-audit to help you find hidden gold in your business. Unleash your Sales Ninja within and let the world witness your transformation.

Winning is not something that happens by accident. Jay attributes winning to a total shift in mindset, sheer grit that he learned from his immigrant South Korean parents, and having a reverse engineered blueprint that actually works.

The Sales Ninja is not just a rainmaker; he's a visionary scaling through sales, leaving an indelible mark on lives and businesses alike. Join him in his mission to impact 1 million lives by creating a billion-dollar legacy, one sale at a time.

EPISODE 32

JAY LEE

Toronto-born Jay Lee transformed from a struggling pastor to a profitability rainmaker, consistently closing six-figure deals monthly, and always leading in cash collected. His journey, marked by the mantra "sell more to give more," propelled him to sell from zero to $1M in just twelve weeks, impacting over a hundred thousand lives and helping his clients generate $25M+ in only twenty-four months.

Beyond personal success, Jay's mission extends to advancing God's Kingdom, combating generational poverty, and fighting child trafficking. Jay's business aspirations span scaling businesses beyond the $100k monthly to $1M monthly, employing the Reverse G.L.A.S.S. Selling Method—a revolutionary approach that shatters sales stereotypes.

A proven track record includes scaling companies from zero to $16M in twenty-nine months, another company from zero to $2.8M in twenty-four months, and coaching individuals from $10k/month, to $100k/month, to $1M+/month.

Jay and his wife volunteer their time at church, leading the musical worship team. He coaches both volleyball and soccer for his three kids, with many championships and an undefeated record in four years in a two-thousand-member soccer organization. Jay has taken last place teams "from zero to hero" numerous times, and continues to do so in the business world by growing and scaling companies.

Sell More. Give More. www.gosalesninja.com

MARY GOODEN

EVERY EXPERIENCE IS A GIFT TO INSPIRE ANOTHER

"The purpose of life is to discover your gift. The work of life is to develop it. The meaning of life is to give your gift away."

— David Viscott

For as long as I can remember, I have desired to surround myself with other humans who have deeply felt, embraced, and allowed their life experiences to transform and lead them to their most authentic self; people like me, who came here to serve a purpose much bigger than can be imagined; individuals with a passion to inspire humanity by sharing their life experiences in vulnerability and truth.

As a soulful leader I am connected to and in agreement with my truth—open, willing and committed to creating loving and lasting change in the world. By simply being ME and sharing my limitless gifts. Divine Love has taught me that you must be willing to forgive, to surrender, and to let go of all that no longer serves you, again and again—a daily practice of releasing from old beliefs and cultural conditioning and having courage to see the triumph in trials.

I realize that many people have spent years, even lifetimes, wishing away their experiences, regretting their choices, and lamenting their circumstances. So, I have created Anchor Your Light Academy to help humanity change the lens and look deeply within, to reevaluate their perception and step into authenticity and freedom, defined by me, to live in alignment with your truth and receive the limitless gifts that God has bestowed upon each and every one of us.

I wholeheartedly believe that every experience is a gift to inspire another, to encourage and empower all of us as we live with passion and purpose.

So, what is my gift?

It's such an exciting question that deserves daily contemplation. I believe that there are limitless gifts available to each of us. It's more about choosing which gifts you desire to activate, claim or uphold in this lifetime. With that being said, in this chapter I want to share my gift of Divine Love.

Divine Love is my call to eternal service in complete surrender, also known as *"living my best life"*. A daily commitment to remembering, honoring, and anchoring my deepest desires. Accepting the truth, that I have permission to stand as my healed self, to learn from, share and value every experience. A deep knowing that I am safe, supported, and loved. My willingness to trust the outcome and take inspired action toward my deepest desire, the calling of my heart, and the passion and purpose of my soul.

Unbound

Detached

Limitless

Feeling all the love

Seeing all the stars

Touching all the trees

Tasting all the food

Hearing all that is in harmony

Every day I surrender to this gift of Divine Love.

I feel honored to be chosen and eagerly accept the invitation to vibrate at the highest frequency of unconditional love as the heart of humanity. This invitation was brought forward through my dear soul friend Taryn van der Merwe. Taryn is a gifted & highly sought after Akashic Record Teacher, channel and divine feminine way shower, using her own intuitive medicine of Heartsense Healing™. In case you are wondering, my requirements for standing as a heart in humanity are simple. A promise to claim, create and celebrate my desire every day. And to joyfully support others to discover and embody their deepest desire through Divine Love.

To be called into eternal service is a precious gift. Perhaps somewhere along the journey I "worked" for it, but that doesn't matter, it still feels magnificent, and I celebrate this gift every day by choosing my desire. I have created a daily practice to claim, create and celebrate my deepest desire and embody my sovereignty. This sacred practice allows me to give, receive and serve from a place of complete acceptance, fulfillment, love and trust.

My greatest desire for humanity is that each of you get to remember your own gifts, consciously remove yourself from the loop of duality and embody your highest potential, complete oneness and Divine Love.

This is a purposeful poem I read to myself daily.

Dear One,
I surrender to a deeper state of devotion, my most Divine self.
I am open to receive limitless support in ways I cannot imagine or have ever seen before.
I am open to receive an abundance of creativity, passion and purpose that brings joy to the whole.
I am open to receive valuable life experiences that elevate my confidence, curiosity and trust.
I am open to receive the highest frequency of love, compassion and grace.
I am delighted to shine my light and share my gifts with the world.
My mind is pure, my spirit is clear.
Show me the way today, what is mine to share.

Choosing A Life Less Ordinary

It took everything IN me to surrender – let in a life of eternal service.

It took everything IN me to release the program – that I came here to suffer.

It took everything IN me to remember – that I am Divine Love.

I AM the creator of my life, and so are you!

Would you believe me if I told you that every experience in your life was based on a choice that you made? Maybe consciously, subconsciously, or unconsciously within the vibration of your body. Maybe because of cultural conditions, external pressure or a program. In fact, when I take a moment to look back at my own journey, I can see clearly where I was choosing to lean into the BS that society conditioned me to believe. For me, it was all about chasing the *"American Dream"*. A life that looked great on the outside and oozed with disappointment and resentment on the inside.

Who was I to desire something different or recognize there could be another way?

Have you ever wondered what would happen if you stopped getting angry at yourself for the life you have chosen? If you changed the program and stood on the other side of condemnation? How about releasing from the forecast of failure and surrendering to your desire?

What if you flipped the switch and chose to receive your life as a gift, rather than a burden? What if you made a conscious choice to anchor in faith, joy and love? To shine your brilliant light no matter what!

Have you ever wondered what life would be like if you accepted wholeheartedly that you are safe, supported and loved?

Well...

YOU ARE!

I have spent forty-seven years exploring and embodying the magic and mystery that I AM. Anchoring my light so that I can be a beacon of hope for those desiring to live a life less ordinary.

Imagine for a moment what it might have been like if the first thing you were taught was the truth; your beliefs become your reality. You inevitably create your reality by the choices you make in every moment.

What a relief... right?

That is probably not the first thought that comes to mind when you hear this truth. It may sound more like, I don't have that kind of power, because if I did, I wouldn't have created ____?! Fill in the blank with the challenge, circumstance or experience that has held you hostage for far too long.

Flashback, for those of you that haven't read my stories. I have surrendered to what I call Divine Love. I have let in the very best version of me, and it shapeshifts daily. I have stopped allowing conditioned beliefs, striving for success, and meeting the expectations of others to lead the way. I have released from guilt, shame, and discomfort, both self-inflicted and that which is projected toward me. Every day I remember that I am free to BE.

I played in the corporate carnival for over twenty years to witness the strength, commitment, and courage of my humanness. It wasn't easy and I did everything I could to make myself believe it was fun.

I spent twenty-two years married to a military man. I was the head of household and a mother of two, with all the motivation and determination to create a perfect life. A life filled with love, trust, and prosperity. This was an extraordinary experience, and I wouldn't change a single thing.

And then it happened... My perfect life met my reality, logic and reason flew out the window and I panicked. Literally, I had a panic attack. My energy of overwhelm had maxed out and my body reacted. The truth is, I lost control and was brought to the scared crossroads of my evolution. I didn't respond immediately; I had spent a lifetime building an empire based on doing and not feeling. I took great pride in my ability to adapt and overcome.

It took me a decade to fully allow my brilliance to step forward. The first invitation was that I take better care of my mind, body and heart. I trained, taught, and attuned to the modalities of yoga, meditation, breathwork, reiki energy and sound healing vibrations. I exercised daily, received weekly massages, prepared delicious meals, and created space for more fun & play.

I resigned from my corporate carnival, moved to the south, de-cluttered my life, got a divorce, cracked my heart open, travelled a lot, opened my yoga studio, married my match, and surrendered to a life less ordinary.

Not all of these experiences were easy, but each one was totally worth it. They reminded me that radical self-acceptance, love and trust are necessary ingredients to living a life full of passion and purpose.

Contrary to what you may believe, anything is possible.

I released all programming related to my circumstances and societal expectations and created a new way that fit my desires. I stated the following mantra with conviction regularly:

> *I Love Myself*
> *I Trust Myself*
> *I Am Enough*

One day at a time, one experience at a time, and one mantra at a time I created a practice of radical acceptance, love and trust. I chose to seek value in every experience. I let go of the idea that life was happening to me and chose to recognize that life is always happening for me.

It wasn't until I started writing that I truly realized the power within ME and the gifts that are flowing through me. Being a witness to my life reminded me of who I am and what I came here to share. Writing helped me to see how my actions created my outcomes and that I could choose to see them as a gift.

I believe the human experience is an invitation to discover the very best version of you. The practices listed below support me in holding the highest vibration of unconditional love.

1. Daily connection with higher-self, Divine oneness. In utter stillness with full awareness, I open to receive guidance, support and love. I call upon my guides, angels, ancestors and Divine team. I pray for my family, friends and clients. I practice being fully present in an all-encompassing way.

2. Daily movement and exercise to welcome in positive endorphins and encourage an optimistic mindset. I love to spend time in nature and align with the highest frequency of abundance, nourishment and presence. I surround myself with beautiful things and heart-centered people. I choose to take inspired action toward ease and grace.

3. Daily celebration and gratitude to keep my vibration in the highest frequency of love. I laugh, play, and celebrate everything. I connect with and send loving messages to my family, friends and clients. I choose to believe that I am a fountain of joy and I lead from a positive energy, therefore everything I receive back is a vibrational match.

I acknowledge, accept, and align with the ineffable truth living in the deepest part of me, rather than being bound by hollow definitions and limited circumstances.

I invite you to create a daily practice of choosing to live your best life. The universe is here to guide, love and support your journey to Divine Love.

What does a joyful and prosperous life look like for you?

How can you commit to taking inspired action toward your passion?

Are you willing to believe wholeheartedly that you deserve everything you desire?

Do you trust that your inner knowing is always leading you toward your desired outcome?

Choose to move toward what feels best for you and aligns with your vision of Divine Love. Treat this journey the same as you would a new friendship, get excited about it, prepare for new adventures, surrender to the unknown and have fun!

The Sacred Flow

The sacred flow is all around us, weaving the essence of freedom through every part of our awareness. Through every dancing fire and falling leaf, every blooming flower and flowing stream. We are surrounded by life and its delicate cycles.

We are alive in The Golden Age where dreams become a reality, manifestation instantaneous, experiences are perpetual freedom and there is no ego involvement apart from the higher self.

A time for each of us to live as God, manifested on Earth in human form, in service to the Divine plan, God, Humanity and the Earth.

A state of Pure Potentiality where the universal laws of oneness and attraction facilitate a state where we return to oneness with God, to be love, wisdom and power, to embrace all as an extension of God, to surrender and allow while living from the heart, continually being bathed with the energy of love.

If you choose to allow everything to be in its' true essence, then all is in peace and harmony.

Like a child with a magic wand, we GET to create everything that shows up next! To plant the seeds of our deepest desire into the unconditional safety, support and love that only Mother Earth provides. We GET to share opportunities, resources and truth in beautiful communities. To play, praise and celebrate in freedom, knowing that we are always provided for!

We all get to BE in this life different. Fully supported by our Divine team, where there are no rules and regulations, only invitations and opportunities to shine our most authentic light. Endless ways to share love, grace and compassion. Magnificent ways to create and receive miracles. Tremendous ways to transcend and live beyond the illusion.

So, are you willing to get out of your own way and do things different? To remember that you GET to create your reality.

Everything you desire lives on the other side of the illusion that tells you that you can't afford it, you're not worthy, your life story doesn't matter, or that you're not chosen.

What if it's time to tell a NEW story?

A story filled with acceptance, love, harmony, truth and transformation. A story that serves the world for lifetimes to come.

Immerse yourself in Love!
Choose Love
Choose your Perception
Choose your Energy
Choose your Destiny

Embrace everything that comes for you!
Honor Yourself
Honor your Emotions
Honor your Body
Honor your Soul

Embrace everything you came here to BE unapologetically!

You are the sacred creator of your life; you are the one that you have been waiting for.

XOXO ~ Mary Gooden

<u>Start Your Journey</u>

EPISODE 55

MARY GOODEN

Mary Gooden is an International Speaker, Best Selling Author and Publisher, Podcast host, Retreat facilitator & Business mentor.

She believes that abundance thrives in your ability to remain aligned and authentic, which is a daily practice. Mary has studied and practiced Yoga, Meditation and Reiki Energy Harmonizing for almost twenty years. By taking an intuitive approach, she focuses on creating a space for her clients to embody their true essence through an immersive experience available online or in Sedona, Arizona.

Mary is the founder of Divine Destiny Mentoring & Publishing, she joyfully supports conscious coaches, thought leaders, visionaries, and purpose driven entrepreneurs build bountiful businesses, become published authors and align with sovereign success through her VIP programs that amplify visibility, impact, and prosperity for her clients.

Grab my gift: https://www.marygooden.com/gift

KIM WAGNER

STEPPING INTO YOUR GREATNESS

Like so many before me, my gift was born from tragedy. Losing both of my parents to cancer within twenty months of each other was a horrible experience that changed me forever. At the time of my mother's death, I was six months pregnant with my second child. The grief, fear, and concern about my unborn son's health while I was going through such a tough time was the beginning of both my healing journey —and also the discovery of my life's mission.

Looking back, it was such a time of massive learning and change. There is no way I would be on this path without such great loss, and for that I am grateful. Like all tough times, there are always lessons to be learned.

I clearly remember sitting in the church at my mother's funeral, declaring that I am not a victim, that this will not happen to me. That's where my real story begins. Once I'd made that committed decision, each change from that day forward has allowed me to transform into the person—the healer—I am today.

While I initially started looking at the food we eat, I soon discovered that we are, in fact, holistic beings. Whilst our diet is, of course, an important factor, there are many moving parts in relation to our total health and wellbeing. That is the key to everything; all parts of our body and mind need to be in harmony to thrive.

Throughout my journey I've trained in many modalities which have helped with my own healing and expansion. When my son was around seven-years-old, I learned of a modality called PSYCH-K® which was literally the last piece of the puzzle that I didn't even know I was looking for. Although I'd worked on all areas regarding diet, lifestyle, and energetic healing, the mind was not something I'd known about in relation to our health, wellbeing, and happiness.

Part of my research led me to Dr Bruce Lipton and, in particular, his book, *The Biology of Belief*, in which he explains that our thoughts and belief systems have a massive impact on our life experience. PSYCH-K® is a modality that quickly transforms limiting beliefs and the perception of stress—and the results are lasting.

After attending the basic PSYCH-K® course, I was able to quickly and easily heal myself and my family. All of the negative and limiting beliefs were transformed, and not only that, I was able to heal generation trauma. Most importantly, I was able to help my son. My mother dying while I was pregnant with him had a lasting emotional effect and I'm so grateful that PSYCH-K® was able to heal that and transform his life.

When it comes to our belief systems, most of them are not ours. Up to the age of seven, everything that we see, feel, hear, and experience is downloaded into our subconscious mind and basically sets the tone for our life. All of this happens at a time when we cannot make our own conscious decisions, which means that our subconscious blueprint is not our own, but rather a collection of societal expectations and rules.

Between carrying around what society in our lifetime expects, along with generational trauma that has carried forward, it can sometimes feel as though we are on a runaway train with no say or control in our lives. Knowing that our conscious mind only contributes to around five percent of our life, and the remaining ninety-five percent is from our subconscious mind, you can see why our blueprint is so impactful.

Looking back at my life, I could see that my limiting and negative beliefs were in play for as long as I can remember. As a teenager and throughout my twenties, my self-confidence was low. Even then, though, I knew I was different but fear of being rejected or ridiculed kept me living in the shadows and doing everything I could not to stand out. My true self rarely made an appearance in public. Like most women, I hid in plain sight, not showing myself, not allowing my uniqueness to be known by others. The few times anyone got a glimpse, their reaction was enough for me to pull back again. The unspoken rule was to blend in and be like everyone else.

The trauma of losing both parents so young gave me the insight I needed to break free. As my mother was dying, I declared to never be around people who brought me down and to only do things that made me happy. Life was way too short to waste time on things that didn't make me feel good!

From that day forward, I focussed on positive growth and change which, in turn, raised my vibration. Friendships that did not serve me started to fade away. I removed myself from all toxic people and situations, including family members. Prioritizing myself and setting boundaries was something I was very new to... but the result? Freedom.

Once I began to step out and be myself, every single thing, however little, started to change. It wasn't instantaneous, but with each step I became stronger, happier, and more confident. There is a ripple effect once you start to heal and things just get better and better. I attracted my new tribe, who loved me for me, and I was free to be "Kim" for the first time in my life. I can't even explain how good that felt.

Each and every one of us has a different story and our own generational trauma to heal, which is why there needs to be a unique, holistic approach. In my opinion, this is where modern science has gone wrong. "A pill for every ill" does not fit into a holistic approach. It's time for radical change in the world of healing where we look at each person as a whole.

As women, we have inherited a blueprint that focuses on us being "of service." Not equal to others and having a realization that we will never be enough. This is untrue when, in fact, women are the life-givers and nurturers of the planet and our beautiful feminine energy is so powerful. Once we can break free of these shackles, our true power is spectacular.

As well as looking at the basics of diet and lifestyle, it's time to focus on an area that could arguably have the greatest impact on our wellbeing. Our beautiful minds.

Getting down to the basics: thoughts are the solution that our cells live in. Living in fear, doubt, and anger has a major impact on our health and wellbeing. If we live in love, gratitude, hope and joy, however, there is a totally different experience. To me it's a simple issue—transform the solution that is our thoughts and it will change the outcome of our wellbeing.

Each of us has some work to be done, for sure. The first step is to heal from any past trauma, stress, and grief. Thankfully PSYCH-K® is a quick and easy method that can heal anything from this lifetime as well as generational issues. It can also be done online, so I'm able to help clients from around the world. The beauty of this modality is that we don't need to know the specifics of any generational trauma to heal from it. As humans, we have some very basic emotional needs: to be loved, safe, and accepted. By replacing our existing beliefs with a positive alternative, we are then able to transform and heal both current issues and those in previous generations.

Something magical happens when old blueprints and constraints are gone. We start to step out of the shadows and into a new reality. Twenty-year-old Kim is the polar opposite to the person I am today. All of the insecurities and limiting beliefs are no longer present. All generational trauma has been healed and I've also managed to heal my children and family. Without having so many mental roadblocks, a whole new existence is born. And most importantly, it's exactly how I choose it to be.

Just imagine living your life free from judgment—from yourself and others. Allowing yourself to step into your greatness. Being unapologetically you.

My superpower is intuitively knowing exactly what is required to help people to feel amazing in their own skin, and to find happiness. To heal the existing and generational trauma and allow the expansion of self-love and self-worth into their lives. Imagine being open to all possibilities and knowing that there are no limits at all. We can be and choose anything we want. Literally, the only thing holding ourselves back is us.

For too long we've been told what we should do, how things are supposed to be. The reality is that WE get to choose. We get to be the author of our own story. All of the programmed, subconscious garbage has nothing to do with us. We've never been told there are choices but the good news is that we now get to say "yes" or "no."

Personally, I choose to live a life full of happiness, self-love, and gratitude. To lift my vibration as high as possible and attract all of the good things in life. To find my own tribe, the people who "get" me. The ones I know and trust. I can take my mask off when I'm around them.

This is our life and it's time to start living it by design. Is the road easy? Not always. The first step, however, is always the hardest, and rather than look at the long road ahead, I prefer to take each change, each new habit, every new beginning, and celebrate them.

It's so important to fully live each and every day. Even in the mundane we can find beauty and happiness.

As Viktor E. Frankl said, *"Everything can be taken from a man but one thing: the last of the human freedoms—to choose one's attitude in any given set of circumstances, to choose one's own way."*

If we can move through life knowing we have control over the most important asset—our beliefs, thoughts and perceptions—we will know true freedom and empowerment. In fact, what we focus our energy on very often becomes our reality. So rather than focus on doom and gloom, let's start using our magnificent imagination and begin to dream up our perfect life. Once we see our goal, we can start moving towards achieving it.

Working in a holistic manner, it's easy to incorporate all aspects of health with clients. Whilst food, movement, and sleep are very important, sometimes mindset, stress, and the perception of stress can cause more ill effects when it comes to both physical and mental health.

This is my life mission: to help as many women as I possibly can to heal and realize that each and every one of us has more potential than we will ever know.

When working with clients, we delve into all areas of life—with the first priority to heal any grief, trauma, or stress that is causing physical or mental discomfort. From there, we are able to transform current belief systems from limiting and negative to beautiful and empowering.

The main focus is self-love, self-worth, and knowing that you are enough. I look at self-love as being the foundation of our life. If that is not rock solid then, much like the foundation of a structure, the rest of the building will be a bit wonky. We need to have strong self-love beliefs to allow decisions made to be in our best interest. Once that foundation is in place, the rest of our life will flow accordingly.

Too often, as women, we give so much of ourselves that, eventually, there is nothing left. Societal expectation along with our subconscious blueprint dictates that we put everyone and everything else first. This is something that needs to be rectified, and I'm thankful that it's a quick, simple process with PSYCH-K® as well as my holistic healing processes.

Imagine living your life and having nothing hold you back. No negative thought processes, or reasons not to try something new or grab hold of an opportunity that comes your way. Perhaps try something you've always wanted to but have been scared of.

Imagine being able to move through life being unapologetically you. Not changing for anyone or anything. There is such beauty in embracing our quirkiness and once our light starts to shine, there is no holding us back. We've lived a lifetime of a blueprint that keeps us shackled to societal and generational expectations. The change with PSYCH-K® is super quick and effective but it can take some time to change our daily habits. Often we've done things for longer than we can remember, so we literally have to decide how we want things to be going forward, and then put that into practice. Being able to choose how to live your life is such an exciting time. And the best news? It can be changed whenever you want. Nothing is set in stone and if you don't like it, do something different. Having choices is the key here.

For generations we have kept ourselves small, hidden, and in the shadows. That time has passed. Once you transform your belief systems and take a step out into the light, the journey to find your true purpose in life has begun. It's the most amazing feeling.

Our daily priority must be self-love. Not just changing our belief systems, but including it in our everyday life. Instead of looking after everyone else, it's time to put yourself first and tend to your own wants and needs. Too often, we spend our days with so many tasks and lists for others that we really aren't living. As part of self-love, it's time to rethink our daily existence.

When was the last time you really thought about what you wanted? If you're anything like me, it was never. Once we've worked on our belief systems, we need to start breaking the habits of our normal life, including how we show up in the world. Generally, we do the same thing each and every day, and do it in the same way.

Years ago a coach asked me to describe my perfect day. I'd spent so much time doing for others that I didn't know what I wanted for myself! Imagine always working towards some kind of freedom—either time or money, which is pretty normal for most of us—and not even know what you are doing it for?

One thing that helped me find some clarity was taking some time for myself. My children were a lot younger back then so I would be up at 5am to get an hour on my own. Having some time to myself every day in complete silence made such a positive impact on my life that I'll never stop. It allows me to sit quietly and go inside to feel exactly what it is I need. To journal and read, and explore what I really want out of life. How do you connect with this when you are constantly running around doing everything for everyone else?

Now I know exactly what my perfect day, and life, looks like. I've written it down and think about it every single day. Once we make a committed decision and write it down, we often start to move towards our goal without even realizing it.

We were not born to go to school, get a job, retire, and die. Goodness, the way things are going now, many people aren't even getting close to retirement age before they have a major health crisis. Losing my parents made me realize that waiting for retirement was not a great idea—they both died well before retirement age. From the age of thirty-one, I have squeezed as much as possible into my life, making every single day count. We have no clue how long we are here for and I don't want to have any regrets on my deathbed. It's time to start living NOW.

Make today the day to begin your transformation. A committed decision is the first step to total freedom and, I promise, it's a journey worth taking.

I am eternally grateful that my life mission is to help women realize they are more than a wife, more than a mother, more than a daughter, more than an employee. They are more than that. We all are.

EPISODE 65 & 70

KIM WAGNER

Kim Wagner is a PSYCH-K® Facilitator, International Best-Selling Author, Reiki Master, Intuitive Healer, Speaker, and Educator.

Using her knowledge and extensive PSYCH-K® training, Kim has become an expert in transforming the perception of stress and replacing any limiting or negative subconscious beliefs. This is the key to living a happy, fulfilled life as we are able to work on strengthening our foundational beliefs that center on self-love, self-worth, and self-acceptance.

Kim currently lives in Far North Queensland, Australia, with her family. She continues to focus on living a simple, happy life while working with clients around the world.

Website: www.kimwagner.com

PAYMAN LORENZO

IDENTIFY AND SHARE YOUR GIFTS WITH THE WORLD

WHAT IS YOUR GIFT AND HOW ARE YOU SHARING IT AROUND YOU, AND AROUND THE WORLD, IN THIS LIFETIME?

We all have gifts. No exception. Some of them can be, and are, obvious, so that we and others are aware of and can clearly see them. Then, there are those that are not so obvious and can be hidden, requiring us to dig a bit to unearth them. But one thing for sure is that all of us have beautiful gifts inside us.

Before we even talk about our gifts, however, let's define what I mean by *gifts*. Then let's look at why, at times, we seem to not see our gifts for what they truly are. Once we've done that, let's look at how to realize what those gifts are for each of us, and how we can share them around us and throughout the world.

First, let's define what those gifts are, and can be, for each of us.

What are Our Gifts?

A "gift" can be what comes naturally; something that seems second nature to us. It can also be lessons, wisdom, and things we've learned throughout our life through the challenges we've faced and overcome thus far. As well as realizations we've had as a result of an awakening or an experience that has shaped us and changed our life.

Why Do We Not See Our Gifts At Times?

Now, let's take a quick look at why, at times, we may not see those gifts in us. One thing we all do, without exception, is to not value what comes naturally to us, what is second nature to us. I've lost count of how many times after talking to someone for the first time, even after five-to-ten minutes, I am in awe and tell them, "Wow, that's amazing! This is powerful and needs to be shared. This is your superpower and your gift."

We do not value them because, for most of us, we've had those abilities, skills, and capacity, for as long as we can remember, and as a result of that, they are nothing special because they are simply part of who we are. We take those for granted.

Examples of Gifts We May All Have

Let's say that someone is really good with words and conveying clear and compelling messages through them. That is a gift they've been blessed with. Another person may make anyone around them feel comfortable and able to open up right away. They attract people who open up to them as if they've known them for ages. That's a gift. Or someone may have a contagious happiness that makes people around them happy, smile, laugh, and feel comfortable. Another example can be that of someone who has been blessed with psychic abilities, whether it be clairvoyance, clairaudience or being able to read the energy of someone by just looking at them.

Gifts can also be powerful lessons that we've learned throughout our life as a result of overcoming difficult and painful situations. There's a blessing in everything, even in the most dire situation.

Now that we've clarified what I mean by gifts, and why at times we seem not to appreciate them and value them for what they truly are, let's look at ways to identify what our gifts may be.

Identifying Our Own Gifts

Let's start with looking at our path, our journey in this lifetime. We've all had our fair share of hard and dark times, challenges, heartbreaks, betrayals, or tragedies. Of course, they hurt a lot while we are going through them, but they are part of our journey and our growth, both in the physical world and at the soul level. These challenges, heartbreaks, betrayals, hard and dark times, and tragedies become our Story. Then our Story becomes our Gifts. These Gifts then become our duty and responsibility to share them with others.

As we all know, Life is a School. We come here to go through these obstacles and challenges so we can learn, grow, and become wiser and better as a person. But that's only five percent of the reason we are here. The remaining ninety-five percent, at least from my humble understanding, is that of taking those lessons, wisdom, and gifts and sharing them with others through whatever way is more natural for each and everyone of us so that we can all benefit and create a better, more positive world around us. For me, it's through speaking and writing, with my podcast and books. For someone else, it may be through music, painting, arts, poetry, sports, etc. Find what is the most natural way to share your story, your wisdom, your Gifts—and do it.

The Tremendous Power of Asking the Right Questions

A powerful way to identify one's gifts is by asking the right questions. Indeed, one of the most transformational realizations I've come across in the last few years as a result of my personal awakening, has been that of understanding the tremendous power of questions and asking the right questions. Asking empowering questions instead of disempowering ones.

Prior to my awakening, when something bad happened to me, I used to ask disempowering questions such as, "Why me? What have I done to deserve this? Why is life so unfair? Where is God?" and so on. Asking those questions didn't help me in any way. All they did was to create a vicious circle of negativity.

However, asking better and empowering questions such as, "What is this trying to teach me? What is the lesson for me to learn through this painful experience?" has allowed me to not only save my sanity, literally even saving my life, but also to make me look at things for what they truly are—beautiful blessings in disguise and wonderful gifts.

One way to identify some of our own gifts, whether they may be obvious to us and others or not, is to look at the major events of our life that we've gone through and overcome. Then, ask, "What was/is this trying to teach me? What was/is the lesson for me to learn through that?"

Take a look at every major event that changed, affected, and transformed your life, whether positively or negatively. Usually, and as much as it pains us to realize and accept this, the more painful the event, challenge, and obstacle, the more impactful the lesson, the deeper the wisdom, and the more meaningful the gift.

Look at those events and ask yourself, "What was the lesson that event/challenge was trying to teach me?

I'll share a couple of examples of how asking better, more empowering questions to major, life-changing and transformational events and periods of my life changed the course of my destiny to illustrate the power of that principle.

Back in 2019, I lived in Hong Kong for a year. It was a very challenging time of my life, as after four years living in China, where I was trying to build a business that didn't work out, I (as a result of that) literally ran out of money. For a while, nothing I tried worked. I became depressed. Then, towards the end of 2018 and early 2019, a Canadian friend of mine who was living in Hong Kong and had built a successful business, asked me to come live in Hong Kong with him and help him with his business.

Long story short, I took the proverbial leap of faith and booked a one-way ticket from Hangzhou to Hong Kong on a cold, late January day. Unfortunately, the year 2019 was not a good year to be in Hong Kong as the city was engulfed in massive protests over China trying to take over and restrict the rights of the city and its residents. This affected business, and loads of businesses and entrepreneurs, as well as investments, left the once-financial hub of Asia.

During that time, I was depressed and nothing was working. If it wasn't for my friend's divine kindness and generosity—he let me stay at his place for over a year for free—I would have been on the streets. I was living on twenty dollars per week in one of the most expensive places in the world. My happy moment of the week was going to McDonalds and getting the *Cheeseburger Combo*, which was the cheapest item on the menu. Yet, despite being at my lowest financially, it included some of the happiest moments of my life because I was attending and hosting events, connecting people, and having a lot of fun in the process.

At the time I didn't know it, but now looking back at that period of having literally no money yet being happy and having a lot of fun, taught me an invaluable lesson for the rest of my life. Now that I am awakened, I've asked powerful questions: What was that trying to teach me? What was the lesson for me to learn through not having money yet being happy?

The answer is obvious. At least now. Not so much back then. It is that: *I don't need money to be happy.* When you realize that you don't need money to be happy in this hyper-commercial and materialistic world, then you attain a sense of total confidence that makes you feel untouchable.

If a client tells you, "I'm going to cancel my deal with you," or someone says, "I'm going to fire you," you have deep self-belief that you will be ok—and your answer is a simple yet very powerful, "Ok no problem." An unshakable self-belief and confidence makes you very dangerous as you remove that power from others to control, manipulate, or threaten you.

The wonderful and life-changing gift in that experience was for me to understand that money is not what's going to make me happy. Sure it does help, but it's not what's bringing true happiness into my, or anyone's, life in a true meaningful way. And then, take that knowledge, that piece of wisdom and gift, and share with others around me through my conversations in my podcast and now, in this beautiful and powerful book.

Given that I had run out of money, my credit was destroyed and my credit cards canceled. I had to ask my sister back in Canada to book me a ticket to return back home at the start of the Pandemic. I will never forget that day—Tuesday, February 25th, 2020—when I landed at Pearson International in Toronto, Canada, with only around $200USD to my name as a thirty-nine-year-old man.

I had no idea how to get out of that hole, but I had the firm belief that I would get out.

Then, once I realized that I would be in Canada longer than I wanted to, due to the pandemic, I asked myself a very powerful question, "What can I do that will allow me to do the three things I enjoy the most—inspiring, empowering, and connecting people?"

Listen to that Voice in your Head

In order to achieve that, I had to get another equally transformative and life-changing realization: to listen to that voice in my head, those hunches and gut feelings. As that's our Soul talking to us and our Soul has two main purposes:

- To protect us, and keep us safe and alive
- To guide us to the next phase of our journey in this lifetime.

As mentioned earlier, I knew that I'd get out of that hole but I had no idea how. Then, one summer afternoon in 2020, while having a late lunch with family, I heard a voice in my head say, "Start your podcast." At first, I ignored it. But that voice kept coming, over and over again, during the next week or two. Then, a few weeks later, in mid-October 2020, which is right during my birthday, I finally launched my podcast.

That has been the single, most life-changing decision I have made over the last ten years, if not EVER!

That's where my podcast, **Leaders With A Heart** was born.

Then a year later, in the same setting, dinner with family around the Fall of 2021, another voice came to mind: "Start an academy." That voice kept coming and coming for weeks until finally I acted upon it.

I was slowly understanding the tremendous power of asking the right questions. Then I implemented that by asking the people I was talking to on Zoom calls all day a very powerful question: "Do you have your own podcast?" To which, over ninety percent responded with, "No." When I asked why, they stated three main reasons:

- I do not know how.
- I am not a techie.
- I don't know where to start to grow it.

That's when I had an epiphany and started asking those same people this simple question that would change the course of my life: "Would you be interested if I were to show you how to launch your podcast, so that you can share your story, display your expertise in order to connect heart-to-heart with your exact ideal dream listeners/prospects and clients, and attract them organically? Without cold calling, DM's, emails or spamming them. Even if you have no existing audience to start with?"

I got a resounding YES! I got six clients within the first weekend and over sixty clients in the next ten months.

Needless to say, that that not only helped me get back on my feet financially, but also blessed me and my life in many other ways:

• Overcoming my shyness once and for all, as I used to be painfully shy
• Finding my purpose, my passion, and my voice
• Blessing me with amazing connections, contacts, and wonderful friendships around the world with people from all walks of life and industries
• It's been part of my ongoing education
• It's been an integral part of my own awakening
• Opening beautiful doors for me, such as sharing my story, message, voice, and gifts in books, first as a contributor, then in my own books inviting guests from my podcast to share their story and gifts in them as in this very book.

Fast forward to today, late November 2023, three years after I started my podcast and YouTube Channel, I am closing in on my three hundredth episode of my podcast. In the process, I have showcased three hundred (and counting), incredible individuals with beautiful, inspiring, empowering, and goosebump-inducing stories.

Sharing my Gifts through my Podcast and Books

Through my *Leaders With A Heart* podcast and YouTube Channel, I've been able to do what I love doing most:

- Empower people to share their stories, embrace their gifts, find their voice, and share them around the world so that they can amplify their impact.
- Inspire them to believe in themselves and go after their dreams.
- Bring and connect people.

These are some of my gifts—and my podcast and YouTube channel, and now my books, have provided me and blessed me with the platform to do so in a way that is meaningful and inspiring for others. My motto when I started my podcast was, still is, and will always be: "Inspiring heart-centered entrepreneurs with a beautiful heart, powerful message, and inspiring story to win."

We all have a story, a voice, a purpose, and gifts inside us. By sharing your story, your voice, and your gifts, you are helping others, and each other, to rise—individually and collectively. So let's share our wonderful gifts, both those that are clear and obvious and those that may be laying dormant inside us.

Always remember that your story, your gifts, are wonderful gifts to the person who is one, two, or at most, three steps behind you. The person who may be going through what you are going, or have gone, through. Just like someone else's story and gifts, they have been a gift, a light, and an inspiration for you when you needed it. It all comes back in circles. We learn from each other all the time. We are all connected. We are all ONE.

Ultimately, your story, voice, and Gifts, matter. You matter. Take a closer look at your life and path so far so that you can identify your own gifts. Then, find what is the most natural for you to share around yourself and the world. Share them in an authentic way, from the heart. The more authentic, the deeper the connection, and the more your gift will inspire and empower others.

So what are YOUR GIFTS? And how are you sharing them around you and around the world in this lifetime?

I'd love to connect with you and invite you to share your powerful story and gifts in my podcast in the near future. And who knows, if your story is truly a goosebump-inducing one, you could be invited to share it in a next edition of the *Leaders With A Heart* multi-author series.

EPISODE 100, 283 & 300
PAYMAN LORENZO

An International Impact Driven Entrepreneur, Payman Lorenzo is a Humanist, Connector, Cheerleader, Podcaster, and #1 International Best-Selling Author who is a strong advocate of building impactful businesses.

As the founder and host of the *Leaders With A Heart* podcast, Payman showcases heart-centered entrepreneurs who are building impactful businesses, in order to inspire other entrepreneurs to do the same. He loves to help, connect, and empower people to go after their dreams and share their transformational stories. Podcasting has changed and blessed his life in many ways, most impactful of all, finding his Voice.

Payman is on a mission to empower heart-centered entrepreneurs to launch and monetize their Podcast and Youtube Channel even if they have no existing audience to start with and without spamming or ad spend, in order to share their gifts with the world, connect and attract organically with their exact ideal audience.

Payman is a Canadian Expat, having lived in fourteen countries on four continents, and speaking six languages, he is currently based in Kuala Lumpur, Malaysia."

Connect with Payman: https://www.facebook.com/PaymanLorenzo

ANAIIS SALLES

LOVE YOUR YES AND LIVE IT!

On the first day of first grade, I could already read and write. In fact, the top digit of my third finger on my right hand still slants to the right from the pressure of my young fingers gripping pencils, pens, crayons, and chalk—anything young hands can use to write and make art. The joy and power of words and creative expression have been an essential part of learning to lead with my heart.

What are my Unique Gifts?

Healing touch. Moving healing energies like a conductor leads a symphony orchestra. Listening with transformative compassion. A vivid, rich imagination. Connection to nature, water play, gardening, and beekeeping.

At age twenty-five, I healed myself of inoperable secondary infertility. With no complications from clearing two completely blocked fallopian tubes, I gave birth to another child.

My body had paid the price of three years of an undiagnosed illness and almost dying of an opportunistic secondary infection. Fortunately, a medication was available that cured that systemic fungal infection. A pill a day for a full year restored my kidney function, but no surefire surgical solution existed that would unite egg and sperm in my womb again without the risk of ectopic pregnancy. My body had generated a complete reproductive system roadblock.

So when my younger, second son was diagnosed with Juvenile Rheumatoid Arthritis at eighteen-months-old, I had already learned how not to be "blown off" by any doctor who wouldn't take the time to look beyond an "if it quacks like a duck, it's a duck" off-the-cuff diagnosis.

A powerful precognitive nightmare prepared me for the experience of my toddler becoming ill in the most memorable and conscious way possible.

I would not allow my sweet, precious, incredibly patient toddler to suffer another listless day in severe pain with a 103°F fever, a mysterious rash on his palms and the soles of his feet, to hear: "Wait until Monday. It's just a virus."

When my son's pediatrician refused to take my concerns seriously I launched into "Mom-leadership"—"We're going to the emergency room now, and if you aren't there to meet us, we'll leave your practice. I know a lot of people and I have a really big mouth." He showed up in the emergency room on a July 4th weekend when he would have preferred playing golf, while our family would have been forced to defer our summer holiday with extended family.

In the emergency room, my baby endured a spinal tap without my being with him! He and I spent a week in the hospital where I watched him like a hawk. High fevers led to very scary convulsions. And after inserting a rectal thermometer, a careless nurse was about to sit my baby up on his bum before I yelled, "Stop! The thermometer is still in him!"

We received a diagnosis of Juvenile Arthritis and a treatment plan of twelve baby aspirin a day. *For the rest of his life?* My partner and I were told this disease doesn't go away; it's "managed."

I amped up "Mommy-leading" again after observing that when my son didn't drink cow's milk, he didn't spike a fever. I began to suspect there was an underlying cause for his illness that might be being missed. My intention? To support my son with the best "Dr. Mom" who lives in my bones. The goal? To help him find his way back to full health. So, I started a daily log to note when Max received medication, what he ate, and track the fever pattern.

This is how I discovered that my child had a cow's milk product allergy. After conferring with an acquaintance who was Head of Pediatrics at the Children's Hospital of Philadelphia, I was reassured that removing all dairy products from my baby's diet for two weeks would cause no harm.

And after only two weeks of no cow's milk? The daily fever pattern was disrupted. No fever for one full day!

Four months later, after grinding vitamin supplements, adding them to apple sauce, and then using a red cow hand puppet to entice my son to "open wide and swallow," all that remained of the "arthritis" was a patch of eczema on his left knee. Our son's orthopedist conceded that medical evidence reported that cow's milk can cause an allergic response of pneumonia in some children. He agreed that my "beta test" of no milk products for two weeks was worth continuing due to the disappearing symptoms and the fact his X-rays showed no joint damage. I also learned that whey, an ingredient in hot dogs, triggered an inflammatory reaction.

Max loved hot dogs, and ice cream, and... and... and... so I chose to use the term "boo-boos" rather than the word "no" for forbidden foods. As young as he was, Max understood, took a deep breath, stayed present, and moved on. Amazing awareness for a two-year-old.

The distressing episode in our lives ended on the day I heard a warning, a voice speaking in my right ear. I do have Chinese genetics/DNA, so perhaps it was a wise ancestor guide?

The message? Don't use the Cortisone cream prescribed for one small patch of eczema. Crystal clear, direct knowing from within: "The 6th Law of Cure in Chinese Medicine. The skin is an organ of elimination. If you apply this cream to his body, you are asking your son's body to reverse its elimination function. You are asking his body to take the 'energy' of this illness back into the body and keep it. Use cornstarch on the eczema instead, so that his body can complete its deep clearing and healing process."

I threw the cream away. By his second birthday, after four months, all traces of Juvenile Rheumatoid Arthritis were gone. Today, decades later, my son has no joint problems or any sign of arthritis.

Curiously, several years later, Dr. Lee—a Professor of Acupuncture and Chinese Medicine who attended medical school with my partner and was a frequent dinner guest—took my two hands in his, "You come to China. I teach you acupuncture!" He was serious. Before returning to China, he gave me a set of acupuncture needles.

Source Decides that I am Ready to be Taught

Shortly before my awakening, I pondered exiting my lucrative freelance agency to study acupuncture. However, the Source of being had a different plan: *She will accomplish the same thing with her hands. Her energy field can interact with and transmute damaged flows of energy to restore these flows to their original optimal frequency/resonance, just as an acupuncture needle does. The human body was not meant to be pierced by metal.*

In March of 1989, at age thirty-nine, life threw me a bigger spiritual curveball. This time there was no physical health crisis. Instead, I was catapulted into being a hands-on healer, one who is able to affect and activate DNA, when all my internal and external connections and my not-always-wise heart exploded into a thirty-second massive energetic and spiritual transformation. My soul knocked on my heart and I opened that door within me. Then I walked through it and onto a new lifeline and timeline.

While on a retreat, I received this unexpected gift in thirty seconds as energy flows and waves of light surged through my body. Empathy, compassion, and energetic sensitivity blew up what had been a safe, secure, but emotionally unhappy life with a man who, I had to face, didn't love me.

Dr. Lee was right about my hands, but I didn't need to travel to China to study healing. Traveling through conscious organization of information, my two hands don't need to use acupuncture needles.

Deconstructing a family is a tragic affair, even when two parties are able to do this without physical harm. My intention was always to use extreme caution to part ways from an abusive partner and to keep myself and the children safe. I managed, but the financial loss was staggering.

Big Fast Changes

Two years later. It's 1991. I am a volunteer intern on a critical burn unit in a hospital in Moscow, Russia. Burn victim Sergei requests my hands-on healing support during a debriding procedure for third degree burns on both his hands. Even with pain medication, this procedure is excruciating.

My hands resting on Sergei's shoulders, I watch energy flowing from my hands create an intended nerve block that disrupts pain signals reaching his brain. Sergei is not in excruciating pain. Rather, he is so calm and relaxed that the physician leaves the treatment room to fetch my videographer to capture this on film. This graphic footage is part of my documentary, *Heart to Heart*.

I did not know Sergei had no pain medication before this procedure.

Later that day, the Director of the Men's Burn Ward shared that this doctor had never seen anything like it. This same physician visibly scoffed at my title of "energy healer" when we were introduced. After the experience with Sergei, his perception of what is possible had radically shifted.

Undeniable Proof! I am not in Kansas Anymore...

As a result of many such experiences, I discovered two powerful personal development questions: *What's really going on here?* And... *What if?*

Other gifts that are now on my back burner helped me relate to children and adults. The gift of an emotionally rich, dramatic nature led to directing playmates in backyard theater productions of Greek mythologies, using bed sheets for togas and lawn furniture turned upside down for chariots. I still adore live theater and stand-up comedy.

Growing up in Philadelphia, I had free opportunities to study art and music. After art class, I took guitar lessons. Explorations of creativity through sound, images, music, words; nourishment for the human imagination were key to my learning to lead.

A passionate student, well-educated, curious, and open, by age eight, I could see energy and see through the walls in our home with my physical eyes—something I proved to my mother. After that incident, on Saturdays and Sundays I was off on my own, exploring the Philadelphia Art Museum or our local Zoo, feeding celery, sliced oranges, and apples to my favorite animals —elephants.

As a result of my passion for reading and writing, I discovered that I have what is known as *Eidetic memory*. I didn't have to study. I could look at a page in a textbook and memorize it. When I take a test, I scan through my memory and pull up the page with the answer.

This is one gift, among others, that I decided that my family didn't need to know about. At a time when brown and black people were held in less regard than we are today, keeping a unique gift private was wise.

Which Gifts do I use Most Now?

My first experience in being entrusted with group leadership was when my elementary school classmates elected me president of our student council three years in a row. Despite being excruciatingly shy, I love public speaking, writing, and performing stand-up comedy, or being as funny as I am fierce!

My most precious gift is the YES that powers my life, each and every day.

In my twenties, as a mother, I became a certified *Montessori Educator* for young children. Loving every minute of it, this choice made it possible to be with my son, Seth, every day. I was paid to teach sweet playmates for my son while I worked with fabulous colleagues.

In my early thirties? A loving but strict mother leading a high-functioning, high-stress profession, I clocked in sixty hours a week to contribute to our family's financial stability.

Then Life threw me another massive curveball! My soul knocked on my heart again. I opened the door again. And I walked through it into the unexpected gifts of being a leader/innovator tacked on to energy healing—and orgasmic bliss blew up a safe, secure life.

There was no turning back.

At age forty, life set up the path for traveling to Moscow, Russia, where I was given encouragement and permission to use my healing gifts on critically-ill burn patients in one hospital, and terminally-ill pediatric cancer patients in another.

There followed six absolutely *Amaze-Balls* years of being on the cutting edge of energy healing just as this old/new paradigm began to raise its lighted path into global culture. I traveled the world and changed lives, one by one, dissolving physicians' skepticism by healing one "that's just not possible" patient at a time.

Then my life blew up again! A shocking, devastating blow—a personal loss that took years to recover from. Teaching energy healing led to having a safe place to land as I healed. Making art and writing poetry soothed my broken heart.

In my fifties, through live theater, visual arts and political organizing, I slowly re-entered life and became a servant/leader in Seattle, Washington, with the organization *Leadership Tomorrow*. Artists, corporate heavy hitters, and an impressive group of civic leaders and professionals took on the problem-solution dance with local non-profits. Being invited in while Director of a small community theater resulted in mentoring homeless young people. A short time later, I led professional adults into successfully organizing union and political power for its practical benefits.

Helpful Tips

Be aware of your gifts. Pay attention when they show up! Think about what fascinated you as a child. As your interests and pursuits evolve, blend their essence into your leadership focus:

- in your life

- in your family

- in your community

- in how you share yourself with those who come into your life for a time, a reason, or a season

- in listening with compassion

- in understanding with empathy

- in recognizing how powerfully healing it is to see and hear, and to be seen and heard.

Does your *full-hearted* "YES" spark imagination and conscious co-creation in whoever joins in to support your passionate, playful, and committed endeavors?

Empathy and self-love are expressions of your heart being alive with a sense of grace. Grace excludes judgment, shame, blame or guilt, rejection, or self-abandonment. You're fully empowered to feel every feeling. Feelings and emotions are not the same energy. Emotions are carrier energy waves that make us human, or inhuman.

There are an infinite number of ways to lead with your heart as you engage life in big and loud, small and quiet, gentle or ferocious ways. *What are the deepest elemental touchstones within you?* Cherish the impactful experiences that have made you who you are today. Appreciate your unique foundation for going from temporary change into permanent transformation.

A near drowning incident at five-years-old seared my young heart with this take-away message: *"No one was, or will be, watching out for you, so figure out how to survive by yourself. In this singular moment, utterly alone although surrounded by family, I became the leader of my life and what happens in it, to it, and for it."*

Work through your difficulties in whatever way life presents them. Embrace challenges, however painful and distressing, as growth opportunities. Even the terrifying ones are pathways to leading with your heart for your well-being. Dissolve, resolve, and evolve! Learn to change your energy field and release those stuck personally-devastating episodes of being shamed, blamed, or judged.

Embrace Bliss and Joy: Always Recognize Your *YES*

This is a powerful choice, especially when cruel, untruthful power-plays leave you to carry the burden of life-affirming truth alone. Never give up your sense of innocence, joy, or finding more self-love beyond what has hurt you or tried to kill your spirit.

Be aware that truth is an embodied feeling state. Love your "yes" and live it—eyes open, no excuses. The courage unearthed in every *Hero's Journey* growth has one inevitable outcome. This is knowing yourself without guile or ego. Know what is true by feeling through your wisdom body. Trust your perception of what is not true, just, and loving.

Anything else reflects the world of illusion.

Discern the Difference Between Free Will and Choice

Being in the energy resonance of truth creates a distinct bodily sensation. Truth produces DNA-charged sparks and goose-bumpy chills. Truth is both immensely pleasurable or deeply terrifying. You've felt pure truth in your body at least once or twice in your life; this feeling can guide you toward **choosing being loving** over **being right**.

Being "right" is a mind project that automatically brings in an energy of judgment.

What if you're the pointy edge of the wedge? What if your life purpose is to crack open new awareness? Being a servant leader demands a process of deep self-reflection which includes asking the value of being "right" in any situation.

Here's my short list. Whatever age, race, nationality, or faith, these qualities are consistent in every global culture and race:

1. Develop, enjoy, and share a leadership style rooted in truth, transparency, and trust.

2. Allow your heart to lead with deep, open listening. Be full of empathy for anyone whose situation is of grief, loss, or physical dissolution. Be vulnerable enough to share their sorrow, pain or regret—as a path to healing and co-creating solutions that you may offer—or participate by being both empty and present as you breathe.

3. Listen before you speak, and feel for what is unsaid as you

listen. Ask clarifying questions! Ruffling feathers is a way of removing lice.

4. Learn how to establish and maintain empowering energetic and emotionally-healthy boundaries.

5. Hold space for tracing the heartbeat of your community with a young, tender finger that wiggles, two fingers that whistle a call for attention, and three fingers that touch wonder with gratitude for the gifts that life shares. Cultivate creativity, curiosity, love, light, and heart-centered focus!

Honor your gifts. Nurture your "YES." Know which gifts are best held close to your heart and kept confidential. Now and then, share your gifts anonymously as the hand of the invisible force that is the Source of life.

Sometimes, loving your "YES" and simply choosing to live it can be mistaken for magic.

EPISODE 154 & 298

ANAIIS SALLES

Anaiis Salles is a new paradigm energy healer and product innovator. Salles' original, unique, hands-on healing methods have resolved cancer, antibiotic resistant infections, Long Covid, generational violence, and ancestral trauma.

Healing herself at age twenty-five of secondary infertility, entirely through inner guidance, and then healing her younger son at age two of Juvenile Rheumatoid Arthritis, a powerful spiritual awakening catapulted Salles into a profound transformation that includes all the "clairs:" Clairvoyance, Clairaudience, and Clairsentience.

Salles' documentary "Heart to Heart" chronicles unprecedented physician collaborations in Russian hospitals with medically-validated results leading to speaking at international events and conferences.

A visionary creativity consultant, Salles connects clients in vibrant, high-vibe international communities that offer high level support for heart-centered leaders, speakers, business and professional coaches, and holistic practitioners.

Own your own business? Key to a successful corporate team environment? Salles deftly corrects accumulated negative impact from lack of professional and personal support. Her high-intensity, high-powered clients are empowered to access new flows of abundance that enhance leadership roles without additional sacrifice in their personal lives.

Ordained minister, certified hypnotherapist, bioenergetics practitioner, EMT, life coach, author, poet, Shaman, speaker, and product innovator, Salles is a shy recluse who loves travel, writing and singing Her book *The Living Spiral of Transformation: Discover the Hidden Power in Your Unique DNA* details her life story and spiritual process.

Connect with Anaiis: https://www.linkedin.com/in/anaiis-salles/

AMANDA LINDSEY

SPREADING HAPPINESS: MY GIFT TO THE WORLD AND ITS GIFT TO ME

*H*appiness... such an impactful word! Whether we recognize it or not, its effects are felt daily. On one hand, people consistently bask in the glow of the abundance it provides. Conversely, individuals suffer immensely due to the lack of this glorious gem. And sprinkled along the axis between the two, exist people who live various incarnations of the idea.

Descriptions and expressions of Happiness also vary. One may view it in a private, personal manner and articulate it by singing alone in the shower. Another might perceive it in the context of community and convey it loud and proud during Friday night karaoke. Happiness is such an individualistic ideal comprising copious amounts of separate components.

While this may be true, the concept of Happiness also contains many universals. For example, Happiness is our choice and responsibility. We—both as individuals and the world as a whole—*must allow* ourselves to see, acknowledge, and receive the beautiful gift of joy that exists all around us. For it is *ALWAYS* there, even in dark and destitute times.

Additionally, the decision to *be* Happy ultimately lies in the hands of the individual. People, things, places, and circumstances can bring a person joy. *NONE* of these, however, can *make* someone Happy.

Other universals regarding Happiness pertain to its magical qualities. It is available to anyone, anywhere, anytime—existing in unlimited amounts. Truly a gift that keeps on giving! When a person bestows joy upon another, *both* the giver *and* receiver benefit. Happiness *NEVER* diminishes in value when genuinely shared or given away; it can only multiply when transferred. These mystical aspects of Happiness, along with the more practical universals, link the multitude of individual human experiences and promote unity, connection, and the whole.

So, why this deep dive into the individual and universal characteristics of Happiness?

Because my mission, passion, and purpose are to bring Happiness to the world and myself. As *Spreader of the HAPPY*, a critical part of this endeavor involves acknowledging, embracing, celebrating, and promoting *both* Happiness for the individual *and* the entire planet. It's about the blissful marriage of self and others, and I lovingly refer to it as *Getting into S.H.A.P.E. (Spreading Happiness Across Planet Earth)*.

Before *Getting into S.H.A.P.E.*

Happiness played a crucial role in my life, even preceding my conscious decision to wholeheartedly embrace the idea of *Getting into S.H.A.P.E.* In school, I participated in groups such as Spirit Club—whose sole purpose was to celebrate members of the student body. We'd create posters for pep rallies and sporting events, as well as assemble "treat bags" to recognize various groups or individuals. During holidays, we sold handmade cards and candy grams. My heart filled with delight at the smiles that were created as we passed out presents and surprised students during class!

The joy of contributing to someone else's Happiness followed me into my young adult life and brief professional career. At work, I participated in the birthday club. Every month, each person would chip in twenty dollars—which would afford the purchase of a big cake, as well as a nice gift for the individuals celebrating their birthdays that month. A delightfully delicious occasion, filled with smiles and laughter for all involved!

My favorite way to spread joy at work was *Happy Fridays!* I'd prepare individual zip-lock bags filled with mini chocolate bars for each person at the office. A handwritten message (spelling out *Happy Friday* in brightly colored letters) accompanied the chocolates.

On Thursday evenings, I'd leave the candy on my co-workers' desks for them to find the next morning. It was magical to watch the child-like grins as they dove into their *Happy Friday* bags. This fun ritual offered a break from the stressors of work, allowed for the celebration of the past week's wins, and provided opportunities for connection and comradery in the workplace.

In addition to *Spreading the Happy* at work, I took great pleasure in celebrating and surprising those nearest and dearest to my heart. Birthday cards were a staple and included handwritten sentiments with colorful stickers. Sending out the cards via "snail mail" added to the thrill, for I knew most people only received bills and junk mail.

Christmas, another special time for me to send out Happy vibes, involved an activity I affectionately called *Elfing*. Composed of *all the things* most people dread about the holiday season, I embraced this task with open arms and tools such as wrapping paper, tape, ribbon, and scissors. I would lose myself in the sounds of Christmas music as I wrapped for hours. And of course, handwritten holiday cards would fill the mailboxes of those I loved.

Then there were my *Random Happies*. As the name suggests, this method involved scattering joy for no particular reason. An individual's name may have popped into my head or heart. A whimsical dream may have prompted me to reach out to a loved one. Regardless of the when's, why's, how's, or who's, I ALWAYS responded by creating a little personalized *something* that I imagined would bring smiles to the recipient.

Spreading the Happy didn't always consist of a monetary component or physical creation. Oftentimes it came down to two things: Hugs and Smiles. Giving away my Hugs and Smiles meant EVERYTHING, for I was giving away a piece of myself in the simplest form of love. And somehow I knew one thing— that *each* person positively affected by my Hug or Smile would positively affect *at least* one other person in their sphere. Happiness is *that* contagious!

But then came a time when the Happiness ceased flowing. The Hugs and Smiles were few and far between. *Happy Fridays, Elfing,* and *Random Happies* were nonexistent.

I'll make the long, agonizing story brief. The pain and fatigue of many years of chronic illness, as well as the circumstances stemming from them, had buried my joy so deep that I could hardly recognize myself. I dwelled in a very dark place.

However...

With the help of medication, physical and emotional therapy, various spiritual practices, as well as a soul-searching, inward journey—*Finding the HAPPY in the Crappy*—I managed to pull myself out of the darkness. I recognized that, *regardless of circumstances,* I could be Happy. This realization was a game-changer, as well as a new beginning for *Spreader of the HAPPY* and her iconic Hugs and Smiles.

Getting into S.H.A.P.E. (Spreading Happiness Across Planet Earth)

My S.H.A.P.E. journey began during the Covid-19 pandemic. I noticed the similarities in the human experience between my chronic health issues (of twenty-plus years) and me, and that of billions of people in lockdown situations. Fear of the unknown, isolation, physical limitation, anger, confusion, frustration, sadness, dissatisfaction, and the complete upheaval of one's life in an instant! These common threads linked me to the rest of the world and I felt demoralized.

I desired my connection with the people of Planet Earth to be one of Positivity, Happiness, Joy, and Love.

I longed to give everyone a Hug and Smile to show them I cared. To let them know that even in the darkest times, there were still things to be Happy about. But even if I was physically capable of bringing Hugs and Smiles to billions worldwide, I wouldn't have been physically able. Because of mandates or personal decisions, air hugs and masks took their places in attempts to keep the Covid-19 virus from spreading.

If only there was another way for me to physically share my feelings of Love, Compassion, and Joy with the world...

I awoke one night—inspired by a dream—and grabbed a pen and notebook to create the vision that filled my heart with so much joy. "Hugs and Smiles" cards (their original name) resembled business cards in size, shape, and design. The front consisted of a simple, child-like drawing of planet Earth with hands of various shades of colored skin surrounding it. The words *Project S.H.A.P.E.— Spreading Happiness Across Planet Earth* completed the picture of what would become my logo of *Spreading the HAPPY*.

The back of each card would contain one of five hand-written Happy messages I wished to share with the world: (1) Hugs and Smiles, (2) You Are Awesome, (3) Have a Beautiful Day, (4) Great

Job, and (5) Thank You. I'd package them in sets of ten, two cards of each saying, with sparkly confetti to add that little extra touch of Happy. These little bundles of joy would be *Fun, Convenient,* and ready to be passed out anywhere, anytime, to anybody!

When approaching some dear friends of mine to invest in my "Hugs and Smiles" cards, they (thankfully) declined. Seeing my vision as *much* more than some Happy words on a business card, they encouraged me to form a Facebook group where I could spread my joyful and inspiring messages anytime I wanted, with greater ease and farther reach. They knew, as I do now, that the Happy energy lay inside *ME* and that I needed a platform from which to spread it, hence the creation of *Project S.H.A.P.E.— Spreading Happiness Across Planet Earth*!

Project S.H.A.P.E.—*Spreading the Happy* Virtually

Project S.H.A.P.E. is *more* than a Facebook group—it is a container of International Happiness! All are invited to *BE the Happy, RECEIVE the Happy, GIVE the Happy,* and *SHARE the Happy*. It's a place to connect, inspire, empower, celebrate, laugh, and have fun. And if you're *NOT* feeling the Happy vibe, no worries. We are here to encourage, support, uplift, and cheer you on—because that's what *Getting into S.H.A.P.E.* is all about.

As of writing this chapter, Project S.H.A.P.E. consists of over eight hundred members from fifty-five nations. The countries represented—working together, joining hands and hearts to *Spread the HAPPY* worldwide—are:

Australia, Austria

Bahrain, Bangladesh, Belgium, Brazil, Bulgaria

Cameroon, Canada, Codevoir, Croatia, Cyprus, Czech Republic

Egypt, England

France

Germany, Ghana, Greece

Hong Kong, Hungary

India, Indonesia, Ireland, Italy

Japan

Kenya

Latvia

Malaysia, Mexico

Netherlands, New Zealand, Nigeria, Norway

Pakistan, Peru, Philippines, Portugal

Romania

Scotland, Serbia, South Africa, Spain, Sweden, Switzerland, Syria

Thailand, The Gambia, Tunisia

Uganda, United Arab Emirates, United States,

Venezuela, Vietnam

Wales

I say this *not* to bore you, but to demonstrate how Happiness can truly connect individuals worldwide and how Project S.H.A.P.E. is fostering such connections!

Happiness bridges are constantly being built, as people from different lands "meet" in this container for the first time and then become friends on Facebook. Quite often, individuals discover they have much in common and join each other's various Facebook community groups. Project S.H.A.P.E. *virtually* brings smiles for miles and encourages people to flex their Happy muscles.

Project S.H.A.P.E. not only positively impacts others, it has had a profound influence on my world. For starters, selecting the daily content I post provides great joy. The task is a Happiness scavenger hunt as I scour the internet for images, articles, poems, songs—*anything really*—that might spark smiles, laughs, inspiration, and Happy conversation.

Personally responding to comments and messages also fills my heart with smiles. I do my *absolute best* to engage with each person who takes part in conversations, creates posts of their own, or messages me to chat. In doing so, I have established global friendships that have turned into family! While I may not physically be a globe-trotter (*yet*), Project S.H.A.P.E. has allowed me to fulfill my dream of world travel in so many other ways.

Project S.H.A.P.E. has also offered me a home—an uplifting, encouraging, supportive, and compassionate haven during one of the most turbulent times in my world. In September of 2021 (about a month after Project S.H.A.P.E. was created), my parents and I experienced a devastating house fire in which we lost pretty much all but our lives. Amidst the chaos of activities like finding a place to live, preparing inventory sheets for the insurance company, attempting to learn how my dad was recovering at the burn unit, and searching through donation bags for usable items and clothes that fit, Project S.H.A.P.E. had provided me with a daily dose of Happy beyond anyone's imagination!

S.H.A.P.E. Cards—*Spreading the Happy* **Physically**

You may recall my dream of "Hugs and Smiles" Cards—little bundles of joy with the Project S.H.A.P.E. logo on the front and a handwritten Happy note (by me) on the back. Thanks to saying *YES* and contributing to my first multi-author book, my dream is now a reality! My publisher decided to invest after reading my chapter titled, *How I Got Into S.H.A.P.E.—Spreading Happiness Across Planet Earth*. Aside from the new name, "S.H.A.P.E. Cards" are the same physical way to *Spread the HAPPY*—anywhere, anytime, to anybody!

The beauty in these cards lies in connection—a lovely, intricate web of Happiness. First and foremost is the connection between me, myself, and my joy. Each card contains a piece of my Happy that I infuse freely, joyfully, and with much gratitude.

Then comes the link between me and those for whom I create the cards. Our direct relationship commences when they place an order, and climaxes upon receipt of the playful package. It evolves into an entirely new web of Happy when they decide who *their* recipients of the S.HA.P.E. Cards will be.

Joyful stories abound with S.H.A.P.E. Cards and it lights me up when people share them. For instance, my parents recently returned from vacation where they had met a stranger walking his dog in the street. A S.H.A.P.E. Card was handed out, resulting in thirty minutes of conversation between random individuals. At the end of their enjoyable encounter, my parents' newfound friend smiled and told them—in a *very* matter-of-fact way—that they would meet again someday.

Another adorable tale involves the daughter of my dear friend. She had stumbled upon her mother's S.H.A.P.E. Cards and was fascinated, asking her mom all sorts of questions. This delightfully curious child *not only* decided to hand out the S.H.A.P.E. Cards to her teachers at school, but she also added her very own take on *Spreading the Happy*—including hand-picked wildflowers with each card!

Each of these cards contains the power of connection, as well as a story. I may never know how the majority of these stories end, but I *do know* their origins. I have created S.H.A.P.E. Cards for people in the United States, Canada, Australia, Italy, India, Tunisia, Nigeria, Uganda, Malaysia, and Cameroon. And I Happily await the opportunity to create them for as many individuals from as many different nations as possible!

Spreading the Happy Through Words

My voice provides the most direct path to sharing my joyful messages. By guest-appearing on podcasts, as well as doing online presentations, I use my voice to engage in Happy conversation. Topics typically include: (1) *Getting into S.H.A.P.E.—Spreading Happiness Across Planet Earth*, (2) *Finding the HAPPY in the Crappy*, (3) *Our Happiness Superpowers: Choice and Responsibility*, and (4) *all things gratitude, self-acceptance, joy, and love*. Something magical occurs when two or more people gather to open their hearts, share joyful experiences, and dispense nuggets of wisdom they've picked up along the way. Whether actively participating or intently listening, *NOTHING* truly ignites the soul as a passionate conversation about Happiness!

My writing also speaks of the Happy messages I have bubbling inside. Content for Project S.H.A.P.E. and my email newsletter, *HAPPY Times and HAPPY Adventures in Writing,* afford me avenues to present my joyful concepts and musings in a short, condensed format. Writing articles and chapters in multi-author books presents me the opportunity of a lifetime to bare my heart and soul—sharing Happy vibes with countless individuals, known and unknown.

Through speaking and writing, I aim to inspire, uplift, empower, celebrate, and spread Happiness, Joy, and Love. On numerous occasions, I've received the most heartfelt feedback that I am accomplishing my mission. Oftentimes, however, I feel as if I am the true beneficiary.

The magic of engaging and connecting with people through the airwaves, as well as the simple act of putting pen to paper, fills my heart with Love, Joy, and Gratitude. I can't even begin to explain the warm and fuzzy feelings I receive. But the practical benefits are pretty spectacular, too. Both writing and speaking my Happy messages have drastically improved my self-confidence and have rooted me in my truth—helping me to clearly and authentically express myself in any situation.

Wrapping it up in a Nice, Little Bow

Project S.H.A.P.E., Hugs and Smiles, S.H.A.P.E. Cards, speaking on podcasts, writing in books, *Elfing* and *Random Happies, Finding the Happy in the Crappy,* and *Bringing Smiles for Miles.* All these things boil down to just *one* thing—**I LOVE being Happy and bringing Happiness to others!** *Spreading the Happy* is my gift and I strive to give it away *EVERY DAY* in *EVERY WAY* I can. And in doing so, it gives back to me in limitless amounts and ways that I could *NEVER* have imagined.

So here's to *Spreading the Happy... in ANY and EVERY* way you choose!

Hugs and Smiles

EPISODE 180 & 290

AMANDA LINDSEY

Amanda Lindsey—**Spreader of the HAPPY** and **The HAPPY Helper**—inspires people into S.H.A.P.E. (Spreading Happiness Across Planet Earth) and assists entrepreneurs in maintaining Happy relationships with their ideal clients. She is the creator of International Facebook group **Project S.H.A.P.E.—Spreading Happiness Across Planet Earth** and wallet-sized bundles of joy called **S.H.A.P.E. Cards.**

Amanda *loves* sharing Happy messages through storytelling. A two-time international best-selling author, she writes articles for online publications and distributes an email newsletter called 'HAPPY Times and HAPPY Writing Adventures.' Her speaking endeavors include guest spots on podcasts and online presentations.

Virtually, physically, and by using her voice, Amanda spreads Happiness —with Hugs and Smiles galore—-to anybody, anytime, anywhere!

Her mission is spreading Happiness, but her ultimate "why" is love. She strives to make each encounter as meaningful and joyful as possible. Encourager, supporter, and avid cheerleader, she believes when one of us wins—WE ALL WIN!

When not Spreading the HAPPY, you will find Amanda embracing her own Happiness—writing, BEing in nature, dancing to music in her kitchen, trying new foods, traveling to new places, visiting with loved ones, and hula hooping.

Website: <u>Spreader of HAPPY</u>

TUCKER STINE

I AM NOT LOST, JUST RE-FOUND

*H*arun Yahya once said, *"I always wonder why birds stay in the same place when they can fly anywhere on the earth. Then I ask myself the same question."*

This is a personal reflection on learning to fly; an honest look into my own unpredictable human experience when I was faced with crippling anxiety that led me to coping through self-medicating with alcohol and escapism. It's a raw look into how I arrived at knowing the real me today. A narrative of highs and lows, pain and serenity, but most of all, a story of human reconnection at its brightest, most authentic moment. A gift disguised in some of the toughest parts of my life. A gift worth sharing in hopes that it will empower others to find solace in the least likely of places. A gift of flight that convinced me I no longer had to stay in the same place, settle for mediocrity, or live under the false pretenses of someone else's expectations.

Some of the most interesting and amazing people I meet and encounter are in recovery. When I say "recovery," I mean rebuilding their lives from a point where hope had abandoned them. When addiction, physical abuse, mental illness, trauma, or any internal emotional warzone whose sole purpose is to quit feeling, numb the agony, or escape reality at that moment, is in control. We lose all connection—to our lives, our family, our friends and, most importantly, ourselves. Even asking for help can seem to be a distant impossibility. I guess you can call it a "bottom" in one's pursuit of the ever-famed happy, eternal life.

But what surprises me is the discovery of a shocking irony, a tale of two opposites that somehow attract one another. We've been given the "gift of surrender" when desperation is at our feet. It's rare to see those two words of extreme polarity shared in the same breath. When we are left with desperation, nothing else remains but to surrender. In fact, this could be the only war we can win by surrendering.

Seemingly, the gift of surrender allows us to feel the most emotional pain imaginable, but the importance is that we feel it deep, real, raw, unfiltered, and without judgment. The gift also ignites us with strength, allowing us to let go of fear, shame, guilt, isolation, anxiety, depression, trauma, and failure, and we no longer have to hide or shield ourselves with lies, unhealthy behaviors, and stories that block the existence of simply feeling. Our ability to be masters of disguise can finally retire.

It's this feeling that inspires a catalyst for recovery and resilience; our ability to have the courage to conquer fear by staring at it right in the face of adversity. Surrender and desperation arm us to be real, genuine, and authentic, to explore the deepest of loves, happiness, fellowship, friendship, relationships that matter, connections that define what the God of our understanding wants us to feel, and what we crave and envision the human experience to be.

Would you believe it if I actually said that I was lucky and blessed to have hit an emotional life bottom? I guess you could rationalize that being at your bottom gives you only way to go—that's up, right? Bottoms bring us pain, hurt, shame, and the most prevalent, fear. But there is something totally and incredibly beautiful about the comeback. There's a newness, rejuvenation, reinvention of something totally unexpected and exciting. Perhaps something we can actually look forward to again after having resigned to consistent, persistent disappointment.

I believe many people often overlook the power of the comeback because they live their lives in the middle—a little up and a little down—but learning to fall down, all the way down, to your knees, enables us to experience the miracles of coming back stronger. In personal recovery and healing we learn to never quit before the miracle happens; a sort of spiritual awakening. And when that awakening begins, it's a rebirth of the life you've always imagined you could see, feel, hear, and yearn for. The human experience is not about living in the middle. We learn from our bottom to achieve greatness at rising to the top—that's where true experience thrives.

And when we embark on that comeback, it's more than a personal journey; it's a tribal quest for learning from our experiences, strengths, and hopes on how we keep rising. We feel more, love more, hear more, and our spiritual, sensory way of living can power our soul to create more, be more, and share more of ourselves. Life takes on new meaning as we watch all of those unhealthy feelings dissolve and we become bright spots in our own lives.

Sure, it's an expedition of regaining one's self, but the miracle can also be found in teaching others through our experience. And at the end of the day, we find that connection again because the opposite of addiction is not sobriety, it's connection—that's what we strive for. Connection gives us back our courage, and we find more courage in the rising and honest living. Anyone can simply choose to give up, to lose hope, but that's where a strong leap of faith can set a stage for directing a new episode of life. Faith without work is dead. But not today. I work for my faith and my faith works in me. By all accounts, my comeback is nothing less than the miracle of living the human experience on life's terms, with the gift of surrender.

The choice to surrender has, in fact, been one of the most valuable gifts I have been given. But it is even more rewarding to see how I can help others find that gift as well. It's not enough to just survive, we owe it to ourselves to thrive. I have always believed that our comeback is our greatest giveback.

In 2015, I was asked to address a large group of individuals who had finally surrendered to a life that was no longer giving them a way to live happily and healthy. It's a public declaration I often refer to when I am working with clients to remind us how finding clarity, connection, and community bring us back to where we need to be. And so, I share that with you in hopes it will serve as a gift for you to find meaning and purpose in a time when it's hard to find our footing. It reads,

"We have the choice to become new versions of ourselves. A choice we cannot take lightly. We have the power to leave the past behind and truly face the darkness that once held us back from everything in our path. While we will inevitably stand in fear again, this time it's different, because on the other side of this fear is something we have all been wanting but have never been able to realize.

But with any vow to overcome fear, comes risk. Those risks, however, must be taken because the greatest hazard in life is risking nothing at all. When we avoid or escape "feeling the hard feelings," there is temporary relief, but the suffering will continue. We've been taught that our failures only weaken our character, yet they are our greatest teachers for how we grow, adapt, change, love, and live a purposeful life. It's an incredible act of self-forgiveness. And in my experience, taking the risk and making the commitment to stare fear down have made me free. Lewis Smedes says it perfectly, "To forgive is to set a prisoner free only to realize that prisoner was me."

It's easy to run towards the light because it's what makes us comfortable and at peace. But it takes a warrior to turn towards the darkness and shine a light. This is what it feels like to find clarity. And clarity is what gives us the connection to ourselves, to others, and to our calling. It's been said that stained glass is just like us humans; they are their most brilliant when they are lit from within. Each and every day, we have the choice to take our challenges and mold them into diamonds, to transform wounds into wisdom, and to simply accept what once was as the gift of what can be tomorrow."

So if you ask me the question, *"Tucker, what is your greatest gift?"* I will answer with two words: vulnerable courage. I did not know the importance of these two words sitting together until I was faced with the fearful decision of not living. Now, with every opportunity I can, my mission and vision are to help individuals discover how those two words can change the trajectory of their lives—personally, professionally, emotionally, physically, and spiritually. In today's business world, I have found that much of the human experience has been stripped from how we conduct ourselves, connect with others, and develop business models that are rooted in impact rather than in profit.

Each day I wake up with the privilege of helping thought-leaders, entrepreneurs, and conscious businesses find clarity using the power of storytelling and brand development to design and develop thriving communities. We, as people, are brands ourselves, and we forget that the experiences we have with one another are the greatest tools we possess for accelerating human impact. Stories have the ability to do three things: First, they create immediate emotional connections with other like-minded individuals. Second, they create trust and relatability that intrinsically develop lasting, loyal relationships that withstand the test of time. And finally, they serve as the backbone of core values which propel mission and vision.

I find it most insightful when people connect with the vulnerable courage within themselves to use their own challenges, failures, and authentic experiences to drive business, relationships, and collective innovation that is not prescribed—but rather, inspired—amongst cultures, workplaces, and communities. After all, I am a firm believer that we buy on emotion and justify with logic. And sometimes we jump right to the logic, which often gets us into trouble.

So whether it's speaking on a global stage like TEDx to share your paradigm-shifting ideas, or having the interview of a lifetime on your favorite podcast, or building your own personal brand and business that has the power to change the way we see the world, it's discovering clarity, connection, and community to tell the stories that architect legacies. That's where I find my heart to be.

I often refer to a passage I now have sitting on my desk. It reads, *"The essence of life is not being perfect, impressing people or succeeding at everything. The essence of life is simply making mistakes, learning from them, surrounding yourself with people that love you when you're being yourself, and getting through the failures so you can continue succeeding."* Before I engage with a new client, I read this to them. If they agree to abide by this philosophy, then I know we can work well together. And as we have come to learn, the act of surrender is a lucrative life strategy unto itself, but also an incredible gift.

Before I leave you, I want to share one last rumination on learning to fly again. Finding a purpose-driven, fulfilling life in an otherwise chaotic hell was something I had only imagined in my brightest days. It all comes down to the essence of embracing vulnerable courage. This is what it means for me to be radically authentic. This is what it means to make that choice to surrender. And it was at my moment of an unlikely surrender, that I realized the only thing I had to change was everything. A path I never thought I could travel down.

As Robert Frost said, "*I took the road less traveled, and that has made all the difference.*" It was never about being lost. It was always about being re-found.

EPISODE 213

TUCKER STINE

Tucker Stine helps conscious leaders turn their personal stories into purpose-driven brands so they can accelerate human impact. He is a brand architect, leadership coach, and public speaker with 25+ years in building personal and professional brands, advising nonprofits and coaching heart-centered speakers, conscious-driven businesses, and thought leaders through impactful storytelling.

Tucker is a mentor and catalyst for generational movements that ignite societal change through the power of voice, including advocating for prison reform and at-risk youth. He has helped 250+ thought leaders take the stage, launch businesses, and share global ideas for change, including the highly sought-after TED platform. His clients have been featured on TED, Goalcast, Upworthy, The Today Show, the Sundance Film Festival, and hundreds of podcasts, resulting in over 100 million views. With one goal, to share a courageous voice and a powerful seat at the global table of conversation, every chance they get.

CEO/Founder @ TUCKER STINE + Brand Architects

619-988-5825

www.tuckerstine.com

MARCUS SNOWDEN IBALLIN®
W/SNOW

PLAY LOCALLY...WIN GLOBALLY

But I Did

I know I said,
that I never would.
But then I thought that,
I never could.

But I Did

-Rei En (published 1979)

Snow first encountered this poem at the tender age of seven or eight. Rei En, the poet behind the verses, was not only a published poet but also a modern artist of mixed media. A woman of many roles—mother, grandmother, and great-grandmother several times over—she was the matriarch of her family. In 2022, she added another title to her list of accomplishments: cancer warrior and survivor. To the world, she may be Regina Beverly from Joliet, Illinois, but to Snow, she was simply "Mom."

This particular poem held a profound significance for Snow, who carried it with him for forty-five years. Its author, his mother, had unknowingly bestowed upon him a creative force that would shape the trajectory of his life. It wasn't until later in his journey that he comprehended the potency the verses held, not just for himself but for those who embraced its simplicity.

Throughout his life, Snow found himself instinctively turning to this poem, especially during times of change and challenges. The verses had been a silent companion, subtly influencing his creativity. Unbeknownst to him, it became the cornerstone of his most significant undertaking—the *iBallin* brand, also known as *International Ballin*. This passion project, destined to be his gift to the world, aimed to revolutionize global competition tourism.

For Snow, *iBallin* was a call to "Play Locally... Win Globally." It sought to open doors for individuals from all corners of the world, bridging the gap between big cities and small towns, offering once-in-a-lifetime opportunities for global travel. But to fully comprehend the genesis of *iBallin*, one must journey back to Snow's roots.

Snow's childhood unfolded in Joliet, Illinois (South of Chicago), during the tumultuous years from the early Seventies to the late Eighties. His side of town faced its own set of challenges, though he, in his innocence, remained oblivious. Growing up in poverty often meant not fully realizing the extent of it. Snow had a roof over his head, clothes on his back, and a mother who loved him deeply. Life, as he remembered it from an early age, was good.

His stepfather, employed by an oil and gas company, provided for the family, while his mother, an artist with a penchant for what Snow called "funny-looking paintings,"—later he learned the appropriate category (abstract art)—played a pivotal role in shaping his understanding of the world. One day, at the age of five, Snow stumbled upon a revelation in his mother's art studio—the world of money and numbers. On the back of one of those "funny-looking paintings," he discovered a series of numbers: 2500.

In his innocence, Snow proudly pointed to the numbers, exclaiming, "So you're selling this (funny-looking) painting for $2.50!" His mother corrected him with a gentle smirk, "No, Marcus, I'm selling it for $2,500 dollars," imparting a lesson on decimals points and commas. At that moment, Snow may not have fully grasped the significance of the lesson, but it would resonate with him as he embarked on his playful days. It's worth noting at this time that Snow's real name is Marcus D. Snowden, but only his mother and extremely close siblings and relatives call him "Marcus," for he's known in a couple of dozen countries simply as "Snow."

These early years, Snow reminisced, were nothing short of incredible. Every moment held a certain magic, an enchantment that would later find its way into the fabric of *iBallin*.

Snow, a resilient figure in the early chapters of his life, established a routine that painted his childhood memories with both vivid joy and formidable hardship. Regularly emerging from her downtown studio or returning from art exhibits, his mom, Regina, consistently brought gifts for her three sons. These gifts ranged from coloring books to colored pencils, sketch pads to pencil boxes. Regina's underlying intention seemed to be the kindling of an artistic passion within her children.

Yet, in an ironic twist, her sons never quite adhered to the intended purposes of these creative tools. With a vibrant imagination that, even then, saturated his world with hues of creativity, Snow transformed oversized sketch pads into soaring paper airplanes. Colored pencils, far from contributing to artistic masterpieces, metamorphosed into the raw materials for tridents, spear tips, and notably, cherished arrowheads for makeshift bows used in "Cowboy and Indian" battles and, of course, spearfishing in the creek.

The financial struggles that wove the fabric of Snow's early years remained somewhat concealed behind the façade of these imaginative diversions. Those formative years witnessed the brutal divorce between his mother and stepfather, prompting frequent stays at one of his auntie's houses until they secured a modest rental in a part of town dominated by rival gang territories.

As the sands of time continued to trickle away, the once frequent gifts from Regina's artistic pursuits dwindled, and the toys became increasingly scarce. The era of surprises succumbed to a stark reality where the family's dinner choices transitioned from the more imposing *Ponderosa Steakhouse* (Van, Snow's stepfather, insisted on these steakhouse visits, imposing his culinary preferences on the family and replacing the allure of fast-food joints with mandatory steak dinners), to *A&W* or *McDonald's*, to much less. The days of fancy restaurants and showering gifts were replaced by a stark contrast—a fortunate day might bring a fried bologna sandwich.

As Snow tells his story, the reality of the financial struggle becomes increasingly apparent. Bread and butter sandwiches, occasionally sprinkled with sugar for a touch of extravagance, became a tangible testament to the challenges faced by Snow and his family. The camaraderie among neighborhood kids, all facing similar circumstances, masked the economic hardships they endured.

The backdrop of their house, nestled beside railroad tracks and a creek feeding into the Des Plaines River, provided a canvas for a childhood filled with excitement. For Snow and his peers, the world of railroad tracks and wooded adventures leading to the river painted a picture reminiscent of the 1986 classic movie, *Stand by Me*. In a nostalgic nod, Snow encourages those who may have missed out on such childhood joys to revisit the movie and identify which characters depict you and your friends. If you've never seen the movie, watch it... you'll thank him later.

From his experiences of having little financial resources, Snow had to become very creative and adaptive to his surroundings. The path for many Black kids growing up where and how he did was very limited and well-scripted—on one hand: gangs, drug dealing, jail, or death, and on the other: sports, college, or the military. Fortunately Snow found solace in sports, particularly basketball.

Snow contemplated joining the local gang, even attempting to form his own "pre-gang" with a small group of friends. They were like a fledgling crew, waiting for their time to be initiated into one of the main gangs. However, a brutal beating at the hands of a similar "wannabe" start-up gang and the betrayal of his supposed friends made Snow reconsider the life of a "gang banger." He didn't hold it against his friends for fleeing; he acknowledged that he was slower and got caught.

In the face of setbacks, Snow found opportunities to learn. He turned to basketball, albeit starting late. Between his seventh and eighth-grade summer, a growth spurt propelled him to 5'10" and later to 6', earning him a spot on the eighth-grade basketball team. Dean Johnson, a family friend, intervened, advising Snow and his mother to change direction quickly. She recognized the predetermined paths for kids like him and insisted he join the basketball team.

Dean Johnson played a pivotal role in Snow's basketball journey, helping him with timing his jumps and witnessing his very first alley-oop slam dunk in eighth grade. The exhilarating feeling of accomplishing something not all players his age could do fuelled Snow's determination.

With newfound passion, Snow poured everything into basketball, leaving little room for studying or learning. His skill on the court compensated for his less-than-competent educational level, and some teachers, influenced by his "on court" performance, were willing to overlook academic shortcomings. Dean Johnson intervened again, moving Snow up to appropriate classes, where he struggled academically but managed to pass just enough to continue playing basketball.

Transitioning from eighth grade to high school, Snow experienced another growth spurt, now reaching 6'2". Although his physical growth halted, he cultivated a crucial skill: relentless desire. Snow learned that if he wanted something, he could find a way to obtain it, and what he wanted more than anything was to dunk. He tirelessly trained his body and gained a reputation as the kid who could "jump out of the gym," winning every dunk contest he entered, including his senior year in high school.

His high school basketball achievements culminated in his team winning the *1988 - SICA West Conference Championship*, which immortalized Snow in his high school's Hall of Fame. However, it wasn't all roses for him.

In his freshman year, Snow found himself deemed ineligible to play the second half of the basketball season due to poor grades. It was during this time that a startling revelation unfolded—Snow couldn't read. His reading and comprehension levels were alarmingly low, prompting questions about how he had managed to progress through previous years.

A pivotal figure in Snow's educational journey was Mrs. Sallie. Devoting her extra time, she took him under her wing, tirelessly working with him to teach him the skill of reading. The tragic death of Aunt Annie, also known as Sheena Bates, became a turning point. Snow, alongside his Uncle Blaine, was the first on the scene of her brutal murder. The full details of that fateful day would be recounted another time, but it was Uncle Blaine who expressed Aunt Annie's hypothetical disappointment at Snow's ineligibility to play basketball due to poor grades. As a father figure to Snow, Uncle Blaine's heartbreak coupled with the imagined gaze of Aunt Annie from heaven, fuelled Snow's determination to learn to read, scrape through his classes, and ultimately regain his place on the basketball team.

Although Snow's academic journey was a struggle, he passed with the minimum required credits to graduate high school. The prospect of being the first among his siblings not to graduate loomed until a timely intervention by Leanne Sallie, the daughter of Mrs. Sallie. She informed Snow that one of his teachers had graded the last test on a curve, granting him just enough credits to pass and graduate with his peers.

Despite signing a letter of intent to play basketball at Joliet Junior College, Snow's life took an unexpected turn when he opted to enlist in the United States Air Force. He considers this to be the greatest decision of his life. His military service spanned twenty-four years, taking him to numerous countries and exposing him to experiences usually confined to newspapers and blockbuster movies. Although Snow could fill volumes with his military adventures, it wasn't until a decade into his service that the concept of *iBallin* first crossed his mind.

At the critical ten-year mark, where U.S. service members decide whether to separate or reenlist and set the stage to retire after twenty years, Snow chose the latter and continued to serve for another fourteen years. Reflecting on his enriched life compared to what it might have been in Joliet, Snow realized the need to share his experiences beyond the confines of military service. In 1999, the idea crystallized—upon retirement, he would return to Joliet and establish a youth center. The aim was to provide young boys and girls with a positive alternative to the challenges the streets of Joliet presented.

Yet Snow's journey took another unexpected detour. Instead of returning to Joliet, he took an extra job, joining the U.S. Defense Intelligence Agency (DIA), training as a diplomat and serving in U.S. Embassies across the globe. His assignments included a year in the U.S. Embassy in Afghanistan, time spent in the Embassy in Bangladesh, and the culmination of his career in the U.S. Embassy in Kuala Lumpur, Malaysia. For fifteen years now, Snow has called Malaysia home. Situated on the other side of the planet and as far removed from Joliet as one can imagine.

In the small town of his upbringing, Snow harbored an unyielding desire to contribute something meaningful to the youth, particularly the young adults who shared his roots. Out of this fervor, *iBallin* emerged as his brainchild.

A glaring issue manifested itself on the global stage of tournaments, contests, and competitions; a realization that dawned on Snow with a profound impact. The system in which these events are organized had remained virtually unchanged for decades, a uniform structure that most individuals were intimately acquainted with. Whether one played or competed in sports or participated in a talent contest, the pattern remained consistent. Winning at the local level granted access to the subsequent tier, often at the state or capital level. The cycle persisted, each victory propelling the contender to a larger stage in a bigger state or city within the region. The ultimate goal, the apex of achievement, lay in the "National Championship" oftentimes held in New York, Florida, Las Vegas, or California— the revered hubs of competition. Yet, the ultimate journey didn't end there. If successful, the victors embarked on an all-encompassing, once-in-a-lifetime expedition, their reward being a global platform, invariably staged in Europe or Asia.

The predicament was clear—think about it for a moment. How many individuals from your hometowns do you ever see or hear about competing on a global stage? And how many who have ascended to this global stage can be identified from their hometown? How many do you know, on a personal level, who have graced the screens of televised extravaganzas such as *America's Got Talent*, *The Voice*, or *So You Think You Can Dance*? The answer, for most, is elusive.

The absence of familiar faces from small towns on such grandiose platforms underscored a systemic flaw—one that was not deliberate but rather rooted in three fundamental reasons that people from our smaller hometowns will not reach the global stage.

Firstly, when you win your local contest you are offered a slot in the next level contest. As mentioned previously, this normally takes place across the town or state and requires multiple days to compete. People like Snow just don't have the financial resources to afford such a luxury. When adding cheese to a fried baloney sandwich was considered a treat, an overnight trip to play a sport wasn't in the cards. After all, these contestants only get a "free" entry into the contest. They must pay their own way.

Secondly, the date of the contest can become a huge barrier and block young hopeful dreams to grace the global stage. Many people in Snow's predicament have to work multiple jobs, and often take care of their siblings or elders. The date may clash with a training camp or studies, and oftentimes Snow can recall missing out on many family trips due to basketball summer training camps.

Lastly, and quite possibly where the largest number of hopeful dreams are dashed—it's next- level competition. If, somehow, you have a loving, resourceful mother and an "Uncle Blaine" who can pool their resources to get you out of any previously-scheduled obligations, and they manage to get you to the competition on time, the level of talent at these competitions is unlike anything you've seen. At each level, they get greater and greater until, ultimately, a local contestant comes face to face with a "professionally" skilled individual. There's no chance to advance for almost ALL individuals.

Snow couldn't help but question this inequity. Having traveled overseas to more than thirty countries, he knew first-hand how broadened perspectives enriched lives. *Why should the residents of his hometown be denied this experience?* Time and money, the perennial excuses, were not acceptable to Snow. He vehemently refused to accept this fate.

As Snow delved deeper into these systemic issues, a resolve took root within him. He envisioned a paradigm shift that would democratize opportunities and dismantle the barriers that hindered the ascent of talent from overlooked hometowns. *iBallin*, in its essence, emerged as a response—a transformative force that sought to redefine the narrative and amplify the voices of those relegated to the side-lines of the global stage.

In the quiet desperation of small-town dreams, Snow resolved to challenge the status quo, vowing not to succumb to the limitations imposed by circumstance. The Grand Stage might seem distant, but Snow was determined to rewrite the narrative, turning the tale of unfulfilled dreams into one of triumph against the odds.

Enter *iBallin*, Snow's passion project—a force so potent it consumed every fiber of his being, compelling him to forsake all else in pursuit of giving back to the global communities that had bestowed so much upon him. This vision had germinated in Snow's mind since 1999, a persistent undercurrent that finally crystallized into a concept in January 2020. Despite the initial challenges posed by a global pandemic, Snow trademarked the brand and launched it, only to see his hopes and dreams crushed by the long-term effect of Covid.

Yet, drawing from the lesson learned in eighth grade—to WANT and to persevere—Snow pressed on. The desire to make a difference fueled his relentless efforts to create a sustainable, pandemic-proof platform that not only allowed people to play locally but also offered a chance to win on a global stage. *iBallin*, the manifestation of this vision, became synonymous with *International Ballin*, an international competition platform that is reshaping destinies.

The mechanics are simple: a virtual playing field that extends from your backyard to your favorite social media platform. Participants engage in contests, tag and follow *@iBallinOfficial* on major platforms, and register on their website: https:// internationalballin.com. Snow envisioned a scenario where small businesses, community leaders, entrepreneurs, and influencers would sponsor contestants, bridging local and global participation and giving back to their communities.

The emphasis is on playing and competing. When victory smiles upon a contestant, the *iBallin* team's cultural attaché reach out to the winner to congratulate them on winning and explain to them what they've won. "You've won the grand prize, all you need to do is inform us two months in advance when you want to travel. We'll handle all the arrangements. Two weeks before your journey, I'll contact you again and reveal your travel destination and the contest you'll be partaking in." This seamless orchestration was integral to the partnership of *iBallin* and *Orical Travels Sdn Bhd*, a Malaysian-based travel agency and the symbiotic brand fostering competition tourism.

With this, two of the three major barriers preventing individuals from small hometowns reaching the global stage were obliterated. *iBallin* sets the stage, contingent on the traveler's chosen date, and *iBallin* covers all the traveler's costs, flight tickets, airport transfers, hotel accommodations, even a city tour in most cities. Yet, success on the global platform ultimately rests solely on one's skill and determination at their level (you still need to win). Snow has designed a portal to possibility, a conduit for dreams to transcend boundaries and for individuals to play locally while winning globally.

You might say that you "never would."

You might say that you "never could."

But Snow Did!

Contact Snow below and connect your band and your community with this global movement.

iBallin®: Play Locally...Win Globally!
Website:https://internationalballin.com
Social Media: @iBallinOfficial,
https://www.facebook.com/iBallinofficial/
https://www.instagram.com/iballinofficial/
https://www.tiktok.com/@iballinofficial
https://twitter.com/iballinofficial
YouTube: iBallin®
https://www.youtube.com/@iballin2849

EPISODE 233 & 300

IBALLIN® W/SNOW

Born in Joliet, Illinois, Marcus D. Snowden, aka "Snow," found his refuge in sports during eighth grade, steering clear of the challenges of drugs and gangs. Through his involvement with basketball, he cultivated strong work ethics, goal-setting skills, and resilience to losses—learnings that helped him lead his team to a conference title, be pictured in the Hall of Fame, and win the slam dunk championship.

Snow's path took an unexpected turn when he enlisted in the United States Air Force. Over his twenty-four-year military career, he served in diverse global roles and assignments, including a European tour, Special Operations, DIA, and diplomatic assignments in U.S. embassies worldwide, including a year in Afghanistan.

After retiring at the U.S. Embassy in Malaysia, Snow briefly consulted for a logistics company before launching his passion project, iBallin® (International Ballin). iBallin® connects businesses, entrepreneurs, and participants worldwide, offering prizes such as dinners for two, cash incentives, and domestic travel. In collaboration with Orical Travels, they introduced

"Competition Tourism," providing staycation packages and all-expenses-paid vacations (overseas) to compete.

Snow's aim is to give back to the global communities that enriched his life during travels to over thirty-five countries, and unite more communities through iBallin®. Snow now resides in Malaysia with his loving wife, Claire, a dedicated educator and food enthusiast.

Contact Snow below and connect your band and your community with this global movement.

iBallin®: Play Locally...Win Globally!

Website: https://internationalballin.com

BRITTANY RYCHLIK

IN TOUCH WITH THE WILD SIDE

I grew up with a love of animals. In particular, wolves and dogs, their canine cousins, although I tend to love all animals. If I had to say which animal comes after wolves and dogs, I would choose horses. My mom's cats also have a priority spot in my heart, especially Ranger. But I would never have imagined that my affinity for animals, and the connection I feel to them, would turn into my purpose work and lead me down the wilder side of my path.

I have always had at least one dog. Growing up we usually had one "in-the-house" dog and outside dogs came and went, as they tend to do out in the country, where I grew up and still live today. The neighbors' dogs come running when they hear my vehicle driving down the road, and if they see me walking, they join me for some love and attention.

One of my gifts is being a *transmuter*. This means that I am always transmuting the energy around me; animals naturally do this as well. It is one of the "pulls" we share, the animals and I, which I like to think of as a type of bond or connection. Have you ever felt your mood or "spirit" lifting, or felt lighter after having been around a particular person or animal? In a nutshell, that is transmuting. With this gift, I do not have to think about it or try to do anything; I just am. But I do take care that I do not keep the energy from others or animals around me. I make sure I remain a "pass through" for the energy so I do not start to feel heavy or yucky.

You might be wondering how I started on this journey. It began with my realization that I had lost myself, my individual being, to the various roles I play—mom, wife, boss (at work), daughter, etc. I needed to find myself, and with that came the need to discover what more I was put here, in this time, to do. In rediscovering myself, after many "test runs" of things that did not lead me to where I ultimately wanted to be, I landed with a coach I instantly "clicked" with. Since then, the "dominoes of life" have gradually fallen into place.

I started with energy healing work. As you might guess, when going through the certification programs we focused on human healing. With my connection to animals, though, I started working with animals too, simply applying the same practices to the animal beings. After all, animals are just another form of beings just like humans. My mom's cat Ranger, was the first experience I had of working with an animal.

Ranger is such a unique cat, with his long body that is covered in black and white fur. He responds to me so much like a dog. By that, I mean he will lean his head into my hand, and one of my favorite things to do while I'm petting him behind his ears is to touch my forehead to his. This immediately strengthens our connection and is so comforting to us both.

Aside from my favorite form of affection to Ranger, the first thing I did from a "work" perspective occurred while he was standing on top of a patio table. You know how you can run your hand over the back of a cat's body, starting from their neck or the base of their head and down over the spine to the tail? Most often, cats will raise their behind as your hand reaches that area—arching into the touch. So, to experiment, I did this same sweeping petting motion but without touching his body. I held my hand about one-to-two inches from his body and he arched into my hand as if I were touching him! He could feel my energetic sweep and responded to the invisible touch. I do not need the visual cues to let me know that I am doing the work, but they are nice in the beginning purely for the visual confirmation.

I continued with my practices of healing for humans, not really thinking too much about making a focus of healing animals. Then I got a frantic call from my mom. She asked that I come over because Critter, Ranger's brother cat, was dying. We knew that this would happen because Critter had been diagnosed with an inoperable tumor mass on his throat. The vet had prepared us for what was to come and Critter led a very happy and comfortable life until his dying day. There was no pain as the tumor progressed, otherwise we would have recognized this and made the ultimate decision a lot of pet owners have to make, which is one of pure selflessness. But on this day, I came over in a hurry and my mom said that Critter cat was in his bed on the patio. Now this was summertime in south Texas, so it was hot as all get out, especially on the patio. I found Critter in his bed, clearly struggling to breathe as the mass had become so big it was obstructing his airway.

This is not a tale of a miraculous cure of cancer. No, this is one of the grace and ease in his transition. When I was rushing over, I did not know what I was going to be doing that day, or in that moment. I led with my intuition and let my heart and Source (some call it God or the Universe) flow through me to help Critter-cat in the way that was most needed. I connected with Critter, not by touch but by energy. Sitting there with him, hunched over, partially under the card table so I could hold my hands just above his body as he lay in his beloved bed, I began to encircle energy around us, allowing energy to flow through me and into him for comfort and pure love. My intention was to ease his suffering and to communicate to him that it was okay to let go and be free.

As I was doing this my body became hot, as is typical, but to an extreme level. My mom walked into the patio and said, "You look sunburned, are you okay?" I replied that I was fine and that it was just the energy work that was causing me to flush red and be hot. She remained there for another minute or so before I told her it would be better if she sat on the breezeway because I was starting to feel Critter more than just his energy, and I did not want her to be alarmed. I began to breathe as Critter was breathing, which was a very labored, shallow pattern of breathing. It became very hard for me to breathe but I was not alarmed. In my rediscovery of self, I had learned part of my gifts is being highly sensitive and empathic to those I serve, and those I am close with, even when not serving. I knew I am an embodier and a feeler, so the fact that I was breathing as if I was Critter did not cause me to panic. The heat in me increased and my skin became more flushed, but I kept working with him and talking to him (in my mind's eye) to allow him the grace to transition.

As I continued with him I became flooded with his emotions. I felt so sad and tears poured down my cheeks. I knew through another of my gifts—*knowingness*—that he was sad to be leaving Ranger. Critter was not ready to leave him, so I reassured him that it was okay, and that Ranger would be deeply loved through the loss of his brother and he would also be okay. I kept this flow of loving and comforting energy going for about forty-five minutes and was there with Critter as he transitioned; in that moment, my breath became my own again. I felt a deep knowing that I needed to lay him in the sun for a moment, so gently and with great care, I lifted him, wrapped him in his blanket, and took him to the sun in the backyard. I laid him down and uncovered his feet so the sun could touch him for a moment. Then I wrapped him back up and placed him in the box my mom had prepared for him while I was with him in transition.

I walked away from that experience feeling all the things you would expect: sadness, relief, gratitude to have been able to serve, and also a little fear that this would be my role—to work with those in transition. Less than twenty-four hours later, I had accepted that if my purpose was to include working with those in transition, then I would do so with grace and gratitude.

This was my first major experience in working with an animal. Now I work with my clients and/or their pets to help them with their traumas while simultaneously easing some behavior concerns. Two clients' pets immediately come to mind— Gizmo and Sandi. Gizmo is the fur baby of a fellow energy healer who lives in Canada. Yes, it is possible to work remotely with clients and pets because energy knows not of time and space constraints. Gizmo's mom spoke with me about his behavior of nipping (biting but he's small so it's more like a nip). We talked for a bit so I could learn a little more about Gizmo and the circumstances when these instances would occur, because it did not happen all the time, or with everyone.

So we set up an evening for me to work on Gizmo and I said I would text her to let her know when the healing was complete. When I do healings, for the most part, every communication I have is with my mind's eye and not spoken out loud, but if I feel like I need to speak something aloud, then I do. As I was working with Gizmo and talking to him, I had a few "knowings" come into my mind. With that information, I talked further with Gizmo about the root issue/trauma that triggered the nipping. I infused more energy flow with love, safety, and security through the communication and the work, and spoke to him about how to talk with his "mom and dad" in a way that did not involve him biting. I felt it was important to acknowledge that he may feel those emotions again, and should that happen, show him how he could best communicate with his mom and dad. After all, biting is a form of communication for animals but, as you can imagine, it is not the preferred way for humans to receive information or the message.

After the first session, Gizmo's mom noticed such a big difference in his lovingness and, of course, the nipping stopped. For several months I continued to work with Gizmo, doing what I call a "maintenance session" once per month, to reinforce the communication we had experienced, and to check in and see if anything new needed to be discussed and worked through. His groomers were pleased to see that he was no longer nipping at them, and his dad also saw the positive shift in Gizmo's affection.

Sandi is a rescue Labrador that came from an all-too-common background of abuse. Sandi's owner is in the armed forces and wears a uniform. He expressed to me that when he had his uniform on, Sandi's behavior changed and she was fearful. She was also not very loving towards him in general. Sandi's owner was familiar with the field of energy work and open to the experience for her so, as with Gizmo's mom, I set a day and time for the session and said I would text him when I was done. While doing this session, I had the need to lean down by Sandi—she was laying down while I was seated. I worked with her and talked to her, as I do, and found that her abuser wore a uniform of some sort and that was why she responded to her dad the way she did. We communicated for a while on this topic, and then I felt a lot of heat by her back end and this "knowing" came in.

I closed the session and texted her dad to ask him if she had problems with her back end; he replied that she did. I told him her abuse involved that area, thus the resulting effects. Sandi's dad said he knew when I was working on her because she started talking in her sleep, which she didn't normally do, so he figured I was "in there" with her. I had to laugh at the way he phrased that, although it is pretty accurate, and it was cool that he got a visual cue from several states away. The next evening, Sandi's dad sent me a picture of her laying across him on the couch! He said she was glued to him and he was so happy.

The last story I will share involves one of my own dogs. Precious, a tiny thing at only 4lbs, loves my meditation corner and will often sit on my mat and be in total peace and comfort. Then every so often, she started to have seizures. The last time, I was sitting on my bed with her and I felt like she was nervous, so I started talking to her. Then her movement became a little stiff, like it does when she's beginning to seize and in a seizure. Now, seeing a person or an animal in seizure can be scary, and you can feel helpless. I *knew* I needed to take her to the meditation corner so I carefully picked her up and cradled her to my chest. I kept her against me and started doing a healing as I walked to the mat, kneeled down to place her on the mat, and kept my hands on her head and behind. Within less than a minute, her seizure stopped! She didn't progress into a full blown episode where her tongue hangs out and she gets so stiff. As soon as I brought her to the peaceful meditation corner and let energy flow through us from one end to the other, she was good to go. I stayed laying there with her for a minute or two and then got up, at which point she did as well and was her normal self.

Never would I have thought I would use my gift to help a person or an animal transition from one life to the next. Nor would I have thought I would ever use it during a seizure. These experiences were not planned and were intuitively guided for me and the animal. I have experiences all the time with animals that are "strangers" to me. A neighbor's donkey got out and after settling him down, he was scared at my attempts to corral him back into the fence. I thought to myself, "rely on the energy and connection and call him to you." So I did and he followed me back into the fence. My neighbor's cousin watched this and said, "I knew you were a dog whisperer but I didn't know you were a donkey whisperer too." I just laughed. I can work with stray, scared dogs and get them to come to me and let me help them. At a wolf sanctuary, I have even had a wolf that was not fond of many of the caretakers, lean up against the fence so I would pet her. The caretakers were floored that she did that and allowed me to pet her. The experiences go on.

I feel so honored every time I can help an animal, whether it is to simply love them and ground some energy while we share our connection, or to heal a trauma. Whatever the animal needs in that moment is divine and in his/her highest good. I will continue to embrace this gift and work with animals and humans alike across the globe; near or far, it does not matter. The work I do has no boundaries—it transcends time and space. Working with and communicating with animals in a way that allows for their best life is a gift I cherish. I encourage all pet caretakers to feel empowered to engage in conversations with healers such as myself, should you feel called to do so. Everyone, even our animal friends, need a little special TLC every once in a while. Those of us healers who walk on the wild side are here for you and your animal family members.

Connect with Me Linktr.ee: https://linktr.ee/brychlik?utm_source=linktree_admin_share

EPISODE 255

BRITTANY RYCHLIK

Brittany Rychlik, the renowned "Energy Ninja," is a transformative force in the realms of healing and personal growth. With expertise as a Geo Energy Healer, Mental and Emotional Wellness Coach, Sound Healer, and Dreamporting Practitioner, Brittany fearlessly explores the depths of human experience.

At the core of her work is the belief in embracing discomfort as a catalyst for growth and self-acceptance. Brittany guides individuals on a profound journey to embody their most authentic selves and manifest their best lives. A lifelong animal whisperer, Brittany has four dogs of her own plus numerous "drop-ins" that visit daily for love, treats, and energy healing.

Inspired by nature and the creation of botanical wonders, Brittany's wellness journey is intertwined with her spiritual path. She draws wisdom and rejuvenation from the natural world, guiding her unwavering commitment to healing and empowerment.

Grab Brittany's Gift: https://theenergyninja.com/free-gifts

LESLIE SLOANE

HOW AN AURACLE CONSULTATION CAN HELP YOU GET BACK ON TRACK

Have you ever been faced with an insurmountable challenge, a deep illness, depression, or a seemingly hopeless situation to which you saw no end? Have you ever wondered if there was any way to truly heal? Do you know the codes that can help you find your radiant and happy self again and continue to thrive? The good news is that healing can be fun! By sharing my journey of self-healing through the power of colours and sacred geometries, I would love to help you find your way back to your own radiance and inner genius. For many years I have worked with healing frequencies that have helped me assist myself, and others, on a journey of profound awakening. It is time for each of us to connect to self-Love and our inner strength so we may fulfill our life purpose and mission. I have seen so many people transform into their colourful sparkly selves, and each story is a beautiful ray of hope for anyone searching for answers.

Today, my primary practice is reading the colours of the soul with a series of colour vibrational cards I created, called *Auracles*. I also make other colour products especially designed for my clients which we discover through a series of colour consultations I offer internationally, both online and in person.

You might ask: why colour? Light therapy has been used by most cultures. Chromotherapy is an ancient concept with very deep roots and is still around because it works. Colour medicine and light therapy was practiced in ancient Egypt, Greece, China, and India. Ancient Egyptians built temples with colour healing rooms. In ancient Greece, Aristotle studied colour therapy. Many healers, mystics, and alchemists continue to work with colour for emotional and psychological healing. Have you ever noticed when walking in a forest how the colour Green calms the nervous system? The practice of forest bathing is becoming increasingly popular. Colour therapy requires learning the entire spectrum, because when our rainbow is restored, we experience happiness, health, and wellbeing. It continues to be a fascinating alchemical journey.

I am very blessed that I was born with the unique ability to see auric fields, other dimensions, and sacred geometric patterns. As a child, I thought everyone was aware of the full healing spectrum of Light and sacred shapes that surround us. Over time, I realized this language of the soul has been largely forgotten. Part of my life-purpose and mission has been to share this sacred art that is so needed on the planet today.

My journey began by taking classes in Traditional Chinese Medicine, Reflexology, Acupressure, and hands-on healing using crystals. However, I intuitively knew I needed another level of education. My life took a turn in 1993 when I met my second metaphysical teacher at the Healing Center of Santa Monica. Ayn Cates Sullivan, Ph.D. was intelligent, colourful, and magical. I knew immediately that she was exactly the person I needed for my next step on the path. During my studies in colour metaphysics with Ayn, my soul lit up and I knew I had found my path. Incidentally, I use the British spelling of "colour" because Ayn trained in England where herbal medicine and colour therapy is still part of the culture. The spelling links me soulfully to mythical Avalon and the ancient healing ways of the British Isles. I didn't know it at the time, but I was in for a wild ride and life has never been the same again.

Over the next decade I learned more about the dimensions of each colour, and how colour combinations form a language of the soul that can be learned. We all have a radiant soul print or "Blueprint," and when we glimpse it, we have the possibility of living a full, joyful, and vibrant existence. The journey also involves remembering our specific geometric design. During this time, each colour offered its medicine to me in an experiential way. Red showed me the soul's strength. I learned more about nurturing and self-care from Orange. Yellow taught me about individuation and sovereignty, and so on. There is usually at least one colour, usually the colour you dislike the most, that will stimulate deep healing. One memorable incident was a powerful experience with the colour Coral. Let me share it with you so you can begin to understand the power of colour healing.

In 1999, I began manifesting hot fluid in my ears that turned the inside of my ears vibrant Red. For four years, I went to my Chinese doctor, took herbs, and engaged in alternative healing methods. Although I felt better, nothing changed the level of fluid or burning in my ears. As a last resort I turned to conventional medicine—which made it worse, so I stopped. I remember working with certain colours that continued coming up, and had a few very profound sessions with Ayn. What surfaced through particular colours were messages from my soul advising me to step away from my mother and take a year reprieve. I was forty-four, about to turn forty-five and knew something had to change. So I sat down and wrote mom a letter telling her how I felt, and explained that I needed this time to step away to remove myself from the angry frequency in her voice that I felt was making me ill. I felt her tone was hurting my immune system, my heart, and had shattered my nerves for many years. I also told her I loved her because that was the most important part for her to understand as I took my time of refuge.

Almost everyone, including lifetime friends, were angry with me. My sister sent me a hate letter that I burned. I knew, however, that I had to step outside of the family dynamic to begin to understand the false ego-personality pattern that had been created and was blocking my true nature. I needed to understand the language of my soul and who I am as a unique individual. Although teachers can point us in a particular direction, ultimately, we must heal ourselves from a place of our own inner knowing. Intuitively, I selected the Coral colour therapy bottles to work with and began to understand that I had to individuate out of a toxic family pattern that was making me ill. I did not know how I would do this, but I trusted the colours and so I continued on my healing journey.

I used a Coral essence on my physical body, and allowed myself to use the intuitive skills that have always been mine to give birth to my true Self. I intuitively used other colours, and noticed as they raised my awareness, shifting my consciousness into a higher realm. I also had a shift internally and I felt stronger. Three days prior to my forty-fifth birthday, I individuated, deciding to mail the letter I wrote to my mom. My ears *instantly* cleared up, and they have been clear for twenty years now. The healing happens when we awaken to a deeper truth which guides us to the answer only we can understand, as it is not in anyone else's Blueprint but ours, because we are all unique individuals.

Coral is used in colour therapy to heal the feeling of betrayal and issues with unrequited Love. The variations of colours that I personally chose guided me to stand up for myself and do what was right for me, instead of doing things to please others due to lack of self-worth. In doing so, I broke a long-standing pattern of dependency that was interfering with my evolutionary process. It was, in fact, a psychosomatic illness that only I could cure by becoming self-realized in my actions. The Coral helped me to align with my true nature, bringing healing and restoration. It was a combination of feeling powerful, sad from having to say goodbye to Mom for a little while, yet feeling the excitement of the freedom that my soul needed. The Coral helped me give birth to myself in my own way and in my own sacred space. Since that time, I have helped people select their special colour or colour combinations so that they can individuate and step into the truth of who they are also. One of my great joys is seeing the smile cross someone's lips and their eyes fill with light as they remember the truth of who they are. Rebirth is only one step, because once we remember who we are, we have a lot of work to do on this awakening planet. This time of stepping outside the family dynamic helped me see my unique self and also my life purpose and mission.

In 2005, I established my company, Auracle's Colour Therapy™, and have created my own colour tools since that time. I began by creating colour healing waters in glass, heart-shaped bottles with a luminous multidimensional symbol on the front encoded with a beautiful blend of colours, healing prayers, and sacred geometries. These could be felt immediately by many of my clients even before they walked into the healing room. Some would begin crying and didn't know why. It was the frequency of Love being transmitted from the Auracles that caressed the very essence of who they were. What they didn't know on a physical level, is that their souls were already in communication with the Auracles even before getting into their cars to travel to see me. I still make these beautiful healing waters today to bring protection, balance, harmonization, restoration to the physical, emotional, mental and spiritual bodies, and clear spaces from negative energies. Each colour healing water has a blend of many sacred oils and colours which go back into the eleventh century. I use no chemicals as they lower the frequency of anything they are used in, and cannot sustain the energy or sound of Love which is the healing vibration required. The sacred geometries I've encoded into the symbol along with the prayers and colours each have their own significant power to help us align physically, emotionally, mentally, and spiritually with the consciousness of Love as they are all the fundamental building blocks of the Universe. Each colour and geometric shape is a code carrying unique information for our human evolution. Collectively when blended, they create a portal of dimensions in which we can travel within ourselves to find the answers we seek.

In 2006 I traveled to Egypt after finishing my first book *Auracle's Colour Therapy: The Power of Love Through Colour*. While there, I received guidance in Cheops (the Great Pyramid) to begin creating the next level of Auracles which looked like cards, but for those with an awakening light body, they can be used as doorways of light codes that can positively influence the human soul. The Auracles took seven years to birth because they are frequency-based, transmitting the Sound of Creation which can be felt dimensionally in the physical, emotional, mental, and spiritual bodies.

I invite you to book an Auracle healing session with me and begin your own unique process of individuation. This does not always mean breaking away from our family of origin, because we all have unique situations. Working with the colours will help you see your own full spectrum Blueprint and remind you of your own unique life purpose and mission. Once we discover the language of colour, our lives become increasingly enriched.

Below are three testimonials from many beautiful healing sessions I've had with clients over the past thirty-five years. Each client describes an awakening and profound transformation that occurred within, and then externally. I share them with you to give you a deeper understanding of how my healing gifts help people, and so you see it from their point of view.

Seeing with Clear Eyes

"When I first came to Leslie, I had a devastating immune disorder called shingles, and I was in so much pain that I couldn't get up on your treatment table by myself, and my left eye was completely red, swollen and closed. During the session with the colours I had chosen, I saw angels around me, and I also saw myself in Heaven surrounded by other angels. This was something I will never forget. After the session was over, I had no pain in my eye and it opened slightly. Leslie is so amazing, for what she did for me. Her words and colours helped me to heal so much in one session, and since then doors have opened up, allowing me to sort everything out in my life. Leslie helped me to see with "clear eyes" what was really happening to me. Because of this, my eyes healed as well. I feel so blessed to know you. Thank you Leslie!"

~ Rosaura Zapata

Out Of This World!

"My session with Leslie left me speechless... so beautiful. I didn't know what to expect or what would happen once we began our session. All I knew was when I met her it was an instant and deep connection. She's loving, warm, and joyous! Her reading was absolutely accurate and actually brought up things from my familial lineage which were plaguing me still, causing deep

pain in my heart. I didn't correlate them at all with my sadness until it came up in the session and I had an instantaneous awakening. I cried and just let it all out. It was a deeply profound realization of something that hurt me so deeply all of my life. I was finally able to look at it and understand what happened as Leslie illuminated my perception. When she did this I could feel everything inside of me change and I felt "Golden," and more neutral I would say. I am so grateful for her... what a treasure! Thank you, Leslie, for the beautiful attunements."

~ Tania S.

Session with Our 3 ½ Year Old Son

"Leslie did a much needed session with our three-and-a-half-year-old son. When he was seven months old, he underwent some tests, for what fortunately turned out to be nothing. However, one of them required he be put under. Upon his awakening, we were with the doctor and couldn't be found for about twenty minutes. When we finally got to him, he was quite upset and it took us some time to comfort him. Later on in his life, he kept awakening with episodes of crying, which I immediately recognized from that moment when he was a baby. He told us he felt alone, like when he was in the hospital. We had been comforting him, praying with him and reminding him that he was **never alone**. I just had a feeling that if Leslie could work with him, it would seal the deal! She came over, brought the colours and "played" with him for about fifteen *minutes. From that night on, the cry was gone! The colours made him feel safe, especially the Magenta which he placed on the headboard above his bed.*

Thank you Leslie for everything... we are so grateful for you!"

~ H.J.

My journey has been, and continues to be, a beautiful kaleidoscope of self-discovery, awakening, and remembering who I truly am as God Source in physical embodiment. Having extraordinary experiences that I'm able to share with others through my healing gifts. is the gift itself. I am beyond blessed, so grateful... and couldn't imagine doing anything else in life. It is my passion, it is my Love, it is my life, and the greatest gift to be able to serve humanity in this way.

We are in a time of great shift and awakening, on profoundly deep levels. I knew this was coming long ago and have prepared for many moons to be here now, and present for all who wish to align with their true "Light." The most illuminated gift of Love to ourselves is to remember that we are Source Energy in which Source is experiencing itself through us. Every thought, word, and deed we procure is helping Divine to expand itself as the Universe, shifting also our internal Universe. By birthright, we are born with our cells filled with Love, Joy, Brilliance, Uniqueness, Magick, and Infinite Possibilities in which to live our lives and create any outcome we wish. All we need is a little help and gentle guidance back onto our path of "Light," which is resonant with every cell of our being. It is then, we will hear our Soul's Sacred Song and remember just how magnificent we truly are.

Golden Hugs and Love,
Leslie
You can book an Auracle session with me at www.auraclehealingcards.com

EPISODES 262, 264, 281 & 293

LESLIE SLOANE

Leslie Sloane is an intuitive Certified Colour, Energy and Sound Healer, with over thirty-five years' experience. She was born with the unique ability to see auric fields, and geometric patterns which are scientifically proven to be the core elements of the universe and language (codes) held within our human DNA.

In Leslie's private sessions, she helps her clients on their healing journeys as she unveils deeply profound truths by using colour and light frequencies which cause an immediate shift in their cells, atomic structure, and overall vibration. This process transforms denser frequencies trapped in the cells which contain pain, suffering and trauma, into higher frequencies resonating with Love, Authenticity, and Joy.

In 2005, Leslie began creating colour energy products which transmit the healing "Frequency of Unconditional Love." Their purpose is to unify all energy fields of the body, mind, and spirit, bringing about a deep sense of emotional and mental balance, harmonization, and well-being.

In Leslie's private sessions, she helps her clients on their healing journeys as she unveils deeply profound truths by using colour and light frequencies which cause an immediate shift in their cells, atomic structure, and overall vibration. This process transforms denser frequencies trapped in the cells which contain pain, suffering and trauma, into higher frequencies resonating with Love, Authenticity, and Joy.

Leslie has offered private healing sessions and conducted Colour Healing Workshops to thousands of people since 1994. Her mission is to continue connecting people to their Hearts and "Soul's Sacred Song" in which they can live their lives authentically and joyfully.

Join Leslie's community and receive a Free Gift!

https://auraclehealingcards.com/

ABOUT THE PUBLISHER
DIVINE DESTINY PUBLISHING AND MARY GOODEN

Mary Gooden is CEO and founder of Divine Destiny Mentoring & Publishing. She believes that abundance thrives in your ability to remain aligned and authentic, which is a daily practice. Mary has studied and practiced Yoga, Meditation and Reiki Energy Harmonizing for over twenty years. By taking an intuitive approach, she focuses on creating a space for her clients to embody their true essence and awaken to their wholehearted mission. Her intention is to activate authenticity, inner harmony, and freedom for as many individuals as possible.

Mary is a #1 International Bestselling Author and joyfully supports conscious coaches, thought leaders, visionaries, and entrepreneurs to build brilliant businesses and become published authors by sharing their powerful story, message, and mission on a global platform. She has created a VIP experience that amplifies visibility, impact, and prosperity for her clients.

She has contributed to fifteen #1 International Bestselling titles and Divine Destiny publishing has created hundreds of International Bestselling Authors.

Mary currently shares her time between Sedona, Arizona, and New Orleans, Louisiana, with her husband and loving daughters.

Thank you for purchasing Leaders With A Heart Volume II. If you enjoyed reading this book, please leave us a review on Amazon or send it to <u>divinereikilove@yahoo.com</u>

The Following Multi-Author Book Titles published by Divine Destiny Publishing are available on Amazon

Aligned Leaders – Sage Wisdom from Women Choosing Their Soul's Mission over Societal Expectation with no Regret

Aligned Leaders

Wholehearted Leaders – Heart Centered Coaches and Visionaries Share Their Wisdom and Guidance on Living Authentically

Wholehearted Leaders

Sacred Surrender - Courageous Visionaries Embracing & Leading In Their Divinity

Sacred Surrender

Revolutionary Leaders - Extraordinary Humans Creating Epic Change On Earth

Revolutionary Leaders

Leaders With A Heart - Global Entrepreneurs Creating Massive Impact

About the Publisher

Leaders With A Heart

Soul Parent - Inspirational Wisdom and Guidance on Navigating Life as a Single Parent

Soul Parent

Divine Love - Uplifting Stories of Radical Self-Acceptance, Truth & Transformation

Divine Love

Soul Love - Igniting the Spark Within

A Collection of True Stories of Inner Healing, Growth and Authenticity to Inspire and Empower

Soul Love

Shine Your Soul Light - Inspiring Stories From Visionaries Paving The Way to a Brighter Future

Shine Your Soul Light

Connect with Mary Gooden, CEO Divine Destiny Publishing:

Website: www.marygooden.com
Email: info@marygooden.com
Facebook: https://www.facebook.com/mary.s.gooden
Instagram: maryjgooden
Podcast: Shine Your Soul Light - Spotify
https://open.spotify.com/show/33HmKCxFNJhAnBZWnrWK0R?si=4338010bbc4f4ee8

Made in United States
Orlando, FL
05 February 2024